ALSO BY ANDREW FERGUSON

Land of Lincoln

Fools' Names, Fools' Faces

CRAZY U

ONE DAD'S CRASH COURSE IN
GETTING HIS KID INTO COLLEGE

ANDREW FERGUSON

Simon & Schuster
New York   London   Toronto   Sydney

Simon & Schuster
1230 Avenue of the Americas
New York, NY 10020

First Simon & Schuster hardcover edition March 2011

SIMON & SCHUSTER and colophon are registered trademarks of
Simon & Schuster, Inc.

For information about special discounts for bulk purchases,
please contact Simon & Schuster Special Sales at
1-866-506-1949 or business@simonandschuster.com

The Simon & Schuster Speakers Bureau can bring authors to your
live event. For more information or to book an event contact the
Simon & Schuster Speakers Bureau at 1-866-248-3049
or visit our website at www.simonspeakers.com.

Designed by Jacquelynne Hudson

Manufactured in the United States of America

1   3   5   7   9   10   8   6   4   2

Library of Congress Cataloging-in-Publication Data
Ferguson, Andrew.
Crazy U: one dad's crash course in getting his kid into college/Andrew Ferguson.
p.   cm.
1. Universities and colleges—United States—Admission. 2. College choice—
United States. 3. Education—Parent participation. I. Title.
LB2351.2.F475   2011
378.1'610973—dc22   2010031864

ISBN 978-1-4391-0121-6
ISBN 978-1-4391-0976-2 (ebook)

For Emily and Gillum

CONTENTS

Introduction   1

1   The Platinum Package   11

2   Rankings Up and Down   29

3   Do It Yourself Admissions   55

4   Put to the Test   69

5   Making the Sale   103

6   Obsolescence Descending   131

7   The Unanswered Question   157

8   The Waiting   181

9   In the Kingdom of the Kids   205

Afterword   225

Acknowledgments   227

CRAZY
U

INTRODUCTION

COLLEGE ADMISSIONS in America is a big sprawling subject, but this is not, you'll notice, a big sprawling book. It's one parent's view, the process seen from beginning to end through the prism of a father's own flesh and blood. (Watch your step—there are lots of metaphors running loose around here.) Like many big subjects, college admissions plays itself out on a small scale. The great issues it raises, the clashing interests and massive institutions it involves, come to earth in the lives of ordinary people, clustered more often than not in families. That's how it happened to us.

It began with a trickle, which is why I didn't notice anything at first. "Who's going to Elon College?" I asked innocently enough, fingering the brochure that arrived in the mail one day. There was no answer, since no one in the house had ever heard of Elon College, much less expressed an interest in it.

"Occidental College?" I called out the next day, when the mail arrived with another brochure—or viewbook, as I learned to call them in the admissions world. "Who in his right mind would go to an overpriced money trap like Occidental College?"

It was a sardonic question, as I'll explain in a moment, and it too was met with silence. On the third day there were two fat envelopes and another viewbook, also from schools I hadn't heard of, and then four the next day, and the next. Within a month, more than a hundred envelopes and viewbooks had been stuffed in the mailbox, glowing with color photos of cheerful undergraduates lounging on sunlit knolls against backdrops of shade trees and red-brick towers. The viewbooks were printed on paper so thick and voluptuous they might have been mistaken for the leaves of a rubber plant—you didn't know whether to read them or slurp them like a giraffe. And each was addressed to my sixteen-going-on-seventeen-year-old son, whose name had somehow found its way onto a mailing list of high school juniors.

My boy was being solicited, as surely and shamelessly as a sailor come to port.

This was something new, something unexpected. I came to see over the next many months that what had once been a fairly brief and straightforward process, in which the children of the middle and upper classes found a suitable college, filled out an application, got in, and then went happily away, returning home only now and then to celebrate holidays and borrow money, has evolved into a multiyear rite of passage, often beginning before puberty.

For some of us, anyway. It's worth remembering at the outset that most American high schoolers go on to college, roughly 70 percent of them, and 80 percent of those attend schools that don't involve the difficulties encountered in these pages. Most college kids go to what admissions people call "nonselective" schools, and many of them begin at two-year institutions; it's not too much to say that there's a seat in American higher education for anyone who wants one. Even the cost won't be prohibitive for the majority of students. More than 50 percent of us spend less than $10,000 a year on college, and a good chunk of this can usually be covered by loans and grants. For lots of high school graduates the pressing issue of higher education is finding the time off from work to take advantage of it.

All Americans, by virtue of being Americans, are winners of life's lotto, in my opinion, as citizens of the most prosperous and least class-bound country in history. But the people spoken of in this book, my family included, are luckier than most. I had a happy childhood. My own children are healthy and don't hate me, or say they don't, and chief among my wife's numberless virtues are tolerance, patience, and good humor. We live in a reasonably safe neighborhood in one of those "close-in" suburbs that have suddenly become desirable. I have a job, as many Americans do not at the moment, and while we're far from well-to-do, the money we bring home puts us, in my layman's reckoning, in the bottom quintile of the lower upper middle class. As a consequence we can entertain a wide choice of futures for our children.

I have no right to complain, in other words. My gripes and whines, my missteps and misfortunes in trying to get my son into a highly selective college are the complaints of a man whom fate has treated kindly. I hope that readers, forgiving as always, will keep this in mind as they go along. In *Ahead of the Curve*, his wonderful book about his years at Harvard Business School, Philip Delves Broughton faced the same problem. How do you chronicle personal misadventures that are themselves, in the large scheme of things, the result of unbelievable luck? Only the luckiest people get to be unlucky in this way. Imagine George Clooney bursting into tears because his lingerie-model girlfriend broke the kitchen faucet in his thirty-room chalet on Lake Como: you will be excused for thinking the lucky bastard really ought to dry up and get over it. As Broughon said about his own difficulties at Harvard, these are high-class problems. So are mine, and I'm grateful for them.

MY LUCK IN HIGHER EDUCATION showed itself early, for I was a college student just as a great transformation got under way. I write about this larger history later, but my own entanglement with it may be worth recounting briefly here.

Both my father and mother were the first in their families to graduate from college, and it was always assumed that my brothers and I would go to college too. Having learned to despise the Chicago winters as only a Chicagoan can, I hoped to get as far away from Lake Michigan as I could and still remain in the contiguous United States. I studied the map.

California!

My parents were obliging, so long as they could afford whatever accredited school I settled on. They had already dispatched my two brothers to the adult world and were now dropping gentle hints that I might want to get my own show on the road too. With the aid of a college guide in our public library—but without *U.S. News* rankings, the massive *Fiske Guide,* the Internet, a single tour of colleges, or direct-mail solicitations of any kind—I applied to three schools in California, another on the East Coast, and a state school in Illinois as a "safety." The only school outside California that I longed for figures prominently in the pages that follow, what I will call Big State University. I had seen it years earlier on a family trip to the East Coast. It was my first exposure to the idyll of higher ed, to the brick buildings and sun-kissed lawns where students drowsed, the blue-jeaned girls making parabolas through the plazas on their bikes, the intoxicating air of postadolescence and preadulthood. I never quite got over it. The school, for its part, was less enchanted with me than I was with it, and I recall the day that the thin envelope arrived, bearing the return address of the admissions dean, as a dark, cold day.

I wound up at the just-mentioned Occidental, in Los Angeles. The next four years straddled the hump of the 1970s, just the moment when the revolution of a decade before was being ratified as everyday life. The insurgents had breached the battlements and settled into the captain's quarters. The renegades of 1968 became the tenure-track assistant profs of 1975 (and the department chairs of 1990). Core curriculums were jettisoned, parietal rules struck down, curfews abandoned. All-girl schools opened their doors to men and all-boy schools welcomed, and how, women; and schools that were already co-ed accelerated the integration of the sexes.

Administrations empaneled student committees and endowed them with managerial powers that would have been unimaginable only five years before. Customs that we now take for granted—student evaluation of teachers, kids sitting on tenure committees—were introduced and soon became standard.

Some people saw these reforms as a major advance for educational democracy. Others saw it as an abdication of responsibility by adults who should have known better. Of the two sides I suspected at the time that the second had it right on the merits, even as I delighted in the indulgences offered by the first.

College life has changed in many particulars since then. The students are by all accounts more career-minded, more mild-mannered, and less politically enthused than we were. Their music is better (no K.C. and the Sunshine Band). Drug use is down, and sexual promiscuity—to use an anachronism that was losing favor even when I was in school—has been hedged in by formal rules governing sexual conduct and by the clinical oversight of health professionals. Still the general shape that schools assumed in the 1970s stubbornly remains, which is why the experience of a moss-back like me remains pertinent, for I took full advantage of the new system as it was then being born. Without a core curriculum, I pursued classes like "African Literature of the 1970s," "Women in Film," "Our Bodies Our Selves for Men," and so on, interspersed with a few dying holdovers from the old regime—survey courses in astronomy, Shakespeare, American literature, and other general-education offerings that, in many selective schools, have since gone the way of the snail darter.

The greater part of my energies were expended in earthier pursuits. I explored the great city of Los Angeles, joined a rock-and-roll band, became a regular at a Zen temple, attended concerts without number, swooned through doomed romances, and pursued a dozen other forms of fun that had nothing to do with traditional education—and all of which, more to the point, could have been pursued at a much lower cost if I hadn't pretended to be a student.

5

This casual and scattershot approach to the privilege of a higher education—an approach that was widely shared among the non-poor of my generation—intersected with reality only when it came time to graduate. While we'd been busy doing our part, diligently drinking beer and chasing skirts, something strange had happened to the general economy. My classmates and I emerged from school into a labor market limp from exhaustion, stupefied from the manhandling of Richard Nixon, Gerald Ford, and Jimmy Carter. The *L.A. Times,* in physical size, had always been a big newspaper, plump with advertising, but by the late seventies even it had slimmed down from the lack of "Help Wanted" ads. Each sunny morning it landed with a little airy plop on the doorstep of our student housing, from which one of my roommates or I would retrieve it. We would carry it to the breakfast table, sweep aside the crumpled cans of Falstaff, and turn with mounting dread to the classifieds.

This was in the spring. We were seniors about to be loosed upon the world, and none of us had the prospect of a job. As we scanned the job listings, our dread was two-pronged: first, that we might never find a way to earn a living; and second, that we might find a job. As it turned out, only the first fear was realistic. We were majors in the most liberal of the liberal arts: one in music, another in art history, a third in the visual arts (a fancy word for "movies"), and one in something called "the philosophy of religion." And morning after morning the *Times* classifieds failed to yield up even one suitable advertisement. A minimally acceptable listing would have read:

> PHILOSOPHY SPECIALIST—pref. w/expertise in epistemological implications of Anselm's ontological proofs and the lyrics of Howlin' Wolf. Hours 1–5 p.m. Generous sal./benefits. No refs. nec. No exp. nec. Pool privileges. Employer assumes payment of all student loans. BYO bong. Applicant does not have to wear shoes.

Not finding this, we grew desperate—so desperate, sometimes, that we would get all duded up in T-shirts and shorts and visit our college's job placement officer. As I remember her, she was a cheerful woman, which was perfectly understandable: as a career counselor at a liberal arts college in 1978, she had a steady paycheck and nothing to do. At my third or fourth appearance she roused herself long enough to subject me to a battery of "employment tests," of the kind that are no longer in fashion.

For two hours, alone in a cubicle, I typed, I spelled, I placed words in alphabetical order, I analyzed charts and graphs. When I was done she called me into her office. Nowadays, under similar circumstances, a career counselor would take a more positive, therapeutic approach. She might tell the student how "trainable" he was, and how marvelously "transferable" his skills were.

But in the 1970s no one was in a pitying mood. "You must understand," my career counselor said, glancing through the papers, "that you have no marketable skills whatsoever."

So I became a journalist.

LUCK AGAIN. I MENTION MY own experience because it nicely encapsulates a larger confusion I have encountered in my recent efforts to wedge my son into college. While expending vast amounts of money and energy on higher education—both selling it and buying it—we seem not to be sure what it's for.

I hate to generalize (actually, I love to generalize) but I think that Americans, as a practical people, are most excited about getting things, a job or a skill or a Wendy's coupon, that can in turn be used to get us other things, a cheeseburger or paycheck, which, in sufficient quantities, can get us just about anything. Whatever it is we're after, we want to make it pay. As a rule we don't get terribly excited about the ineffable. Matthew Arnold, the nineteenth-century essayist, thought up a lovely phrase in trying to describe what people should do when they go to college: learning "to like what right reason ordains, and to follow her authority." Arnold also coined the phrase "the best that has been thought and said," the study of which was supposed to be the substance of a liberal education.

That was his idea anyway. Neither of these pretty phrases applies to what Americans expect from higher education, except in the smallest percentage of cases. We suffer from a built-in confusion of means and ends. We want college (the means) to produce results (the ends) that it wasn't built for. With its ample time for leisure, its relatively light workload, its often leafy setting, its discursive methods of instruction, its vast, comprehensive libraries, college was designed for contemplation, for the slow, steady nurturing of the spirit. It wasn't designed to do what most Americans want it to do: set their kids up to get a good job. If the end we seek is the acquisition of marketable skills, there are much speedier means of doing this than a four-year education in the liberal arts.

What we're left with instead is an entity that isn't the one thing or the other, neither a preparation for productive employment nor an Arnoldian idyll, though it combines elements of both: it's in part an apprenticeship, in part an immersion in the finer things; part summer camp, part group therapy, part booze cruise.

I'M GETTING AHEAD OF MYSELF. It may be that, not really knowing why we want college for our children, we want it even more. But the sources of my anxiety were more immediate. Readers will notice, perhaps, that I sometimes appear to dwell on the issue of cost. It was much on my mind, as it is on the minds of most parents in our situation; and the cost keeps going up. Another cause for concern was the looming presence of the SuperKids. I kept reading about these SuperKids. They figured as protagonists in the innumerable articles that appeared in newspapers and magazines about the craziness of college admissions. A typical SuperKid receives a perfect 2400 on their SATs, earns a 4.3 grade-point average, stars as captain of the football team or the volleyball team, spends summers building handicap ramps in Honduras and weekends curing cancer in the research labs of the local hospital. Some of us spawn SuperKids, others merely feel surrounded by them—and worry about what they might do to our chances of getting our own AverageKids into a good school.

On top of this, I had learned early on that 2009 would be a historic year. A larger number of American kids would be applying to colleges than ever before—three million in all. No one had seen a market so competitive, nor would we again. In 2010 the number declined slightly, and will decline again the year after that, until it stabilizes through the next decade. Even so it will remain at a level high enough to have left previous generations agog, and guaranteeing that our own children will also have the opportunity to obsess about college on behalf of children yet unborn.

A FEW ITEMS OF HOUSEKEEPING: the scheme of the book is chronological, beginning with the onset of the craziness in my son's junior year of high school and concluding eighteen months later when he enrolled at college. (Spoiler alert: he got in!) I've compressed the time line in a few places and telescoped it in others, for narrative coherence and to make it easier on me as the storyteller. All the quotes are real, although you'll see, as I mentioned, that I refer to one school as Big State University—BSU, for reasons that I hope will become clear—and to the little city it occupies as Collegetown. I have assigned new names to two friends and have left others unidentified; when they became my friends, long ago in most cases, I forgot to ask them to sign the release that would later let me broadcast our most intimate conversations to the reading public without getting sued.

And there is indeed intimacy here. It was unavoidable. The subject entangles our deepest yearnings, our vanities, our social ambitions and class insecurities, and most profoundly our love and hopes for our children, with the largest questions of democracy, of equality, fairness, opportunity, the social good, even the nature of happiness. If the book seems to veer recklessly between the two poles, between matters of the heart and the big booming issues of culture and politics—well, that's one reason it seemed worth writing.

The college mania won't subside anytime soon. Too many people, too many institutions and businesses, have an interest, financial and ideological, in keeping it going. This was one of my many discoveries. Though not at all original to me, I took to dropping these mini-revelations at dinner parties, cocktail parties, school sporting events, my office, wherever parents with high school kids gathered. Facing the same trackless future my wife and I did, they scooped up the nuggets like squirrels scurrying for acorns before winter set in, bringing them home to build cozy little nests of worry.

I began getting a rep as an obsessive and, less plausibly, as an expert. Even friends without kids raised the subject of college admissions with me, assuming I'd be interested in whatever news they had. They were always right. And so it happened when an editor friend of mine in New York called me one day out of the blue. He'd read an article in a magazine about a woman I could hire to take all my college worries upon herself and resolve them without fuss. I thought she sounded like a yuppie version of the sin eaters who once served the villages of Ye Olde Scotland.

"But it will cost you," he said. "A lot."

1

THE PLATINUM PACKAGE

What forty grand can buy—Sign of the Turtle—
the marathon metaphor—
the suburban wives meet Kat—
even in the Ozarks?—a pointless scuba class—
from Lisa Simpson to Eddie Haskell—
the importance of the early start—
the chain that leads to (sigh) Brown

FORTY THOUSAND dollars: that's how much it would take to hire one of the country's most notable independent college admissions counselors, Katherine Cohen, for a full-service "platinum package" of advice and guidance that would last from the first starry dreams of ivy-covered brick to the day of matriculation. My editor friend had read a profile of her in a women's magazine. The article pointed out that (studies show) one out of every four students who's enrolled in a private college or university hires a private counselor before applying to school. It's a big business nowadays, this private counseling, a bristling blister sprung from the college fever. Almost all high schools employ college counselors to help their junior-year students prepare for college admissions. In large public high schools, the ratio of juniors to in-house counselors could be five hundred to one, often more. Hiring a private counselor is a way of shortcutting this traffic jam and gaining a quick advantage over schoolmates, friends, neighbors, fellow parishioners, coworkers, and anyone else who gets in our way.

A few things set Cohen apart from her peers. One was the sheer size of her success, another was the sheer size of her fee. From scratch she had built up a huge client base, from across the country and from Europe, Asia, South America. She'd set up shop at a glamorous address a block from Carnegie Hall in midtown Manhattan. As for the fee, it was big enough to choke the most jaded veteran of the college madness.

My problem was that I didn't have it—the fee, I mean, not the madness. This was the first of many financial shortfalls that became acute as the months wore on. I decided to call her anyway. Eventually I got through to one of her assistants, an agreeable-sounding young man named Rod. I explained to him straightaway that I wasn't a potential client, even though my own family was just embarking on the application ordeal. My interest in their work was reportorial rather than personal. What I meant was, while I couldn't pay the $40,000, if he or his boss wanted to share any of their more obscure secrets with me ("Make the Sign of the Turtle in the application photo and the kid will get into Dartmouth early decision") I'd be happy to put it to use on behalf of my son.

Rod said I was welcome to come see his boss speak the following week in Connecticut, to a group of "high-net-worth individuals," as the phrase goes. (This is a euphemism invented by rich people—or rather invented by less-rich people who get hired by rich people—to describe rich people without reminding us how rich they really are.) They were meeting on a weeknight, on the upper floor of the headquarters of a multinational investment bank in Fairfield County, well north of Manhattan. I said I'd be there.

It was a four-hour train ride, and to pass the time I brought a copy of Cohen's book, *The Truth About Getting In*. The cover showed her looking quite glamorous. She had an expensive hairdo swept past the shoulders, accented by diamond-stud earrings. A cream-colored sweater set framed a chaste hint of décolletage. But her eyes were fixed in cool determination, her arms folded in a no-nonsense semaphore. The photo said: pretty, petite, feminine, ballbuster.

The book's tone was the same, friendly but grimly authoritative. Yet its content was a jumble of mixed signals. On the first page she summarized today's seething competition to get into college. It was caused by stubborn demographic facts: an expanding population of applicants and a fixed number of desirable spaces. Toss in the unyielding desire of parents to see their kids get ahead, and you have everything you need to turn the high school experience of countless children into Parris Island. She described the persistent "feeling of scarcity" and "pressure to perform." Innocent high school kids faced the most stressful times of their lives, she said; their parents were about to submit to unprecedented financial demands and experience the trauma of an empty nest.

"I wish I could say it weren't," she wrote, "but the hype is true." Things are just as bad as they say—worse, probably.

"So what can you do?" she went on. "To begin with, relax."

Relax? I'd gotten through the first three pages and my palms were already damp. Our family was beginning to glimpse, dimly, the world she described. I kept reading and couldn't help but admire her technique. She managed to maintain the reader's anxiety at just the right level, a persistent low boil. She was scary enough to keep you turning the pages but reassuring enough to keep you from abandoning all hope and, by the way, abandoning her book too. She drove the reader through a series of switchbacks. When she bemoaned the " 'elite' college frenzy currently gripping America," I thought: Me too! Then she stoked the frenzy. The whole process was like running a marathon, she pointed out. You need years of training, you've got to start early and never let up. Yow: our family was just getting started! That means we're too late? No, she said, with a figurative pat on the head, it's never too late to begin—or too soon. Even now, she said, you and your kid should be making a list of "the hundreds of factors to consider when faced with choosing where you would like to continue your studies."

Hundreds?

High school, she said, "is not a test of whether you can jump through hoops." Then she arranged a daunting series of hoops. There were checklists and calendars to make sure you were on schedule. The implication was that whatever we were doing, we were already behind. But don't worry: get started right away, she added, and "you're already there."

But what did "right away" mean? When *was* the time to get started? It was a touchy question. Fishing around on the federal Department of Education Web site one day I came across a "College Preparation Checklist" for parents and their children. One of the more alarming revelations on the checklist was that my son (and his parents) should have been compiling a "personal portfolio" beginning before freshman year. The portfolio was supposed to contain "game tapes" if he was an athlete, "performance tapes" if he was an actor or musician, and newspaper clippings, statistical charts, award certificates, artwork, school papers, and photographs of whoever he was.

Katherine Cohen's lists were even more demanding. She laid out a College Planning Table showing the courses that college-bound students should be taking, going back to eighth grade. She offered a detailed monthly planning calendar for sophomore year showing what the student should be doing month by month; another calendar showed the plan for junior year; another for senior. My son was a junior. Of the dozens of steps she suggested for sophomore year—going to the National College Fair, "researching colleges," finding volunteer work in the neighborhood, routinely updating a student résumé, taking the practice PSATs, finding teachers who might write future recommendations and sucking up to them, and so on and so on—of all these, my son had done precisely one. *Uno.*

I looked up from the book and watched the weeds and scrub trees speed by along the Amtrak right-of-way. At least he had taken the PSAT. As it happened, I was meeting Cohen on the same day that he was to get news of his score. The PSATs were a big deal, I knew that. The scores would determine . . . well, come to think of it, I wasn't sure what they would determine. Maybe not much. Kids who got the highest PSAT scores could earn National Merit Scholarships. The most desirable schools would tag these same students as their most desirable applicants and lavish them with attention, through cascades of e-mail and those voluptuous brochures. But the effects of a bad score weren't irreversible. A kid could regain his footing by doing well on the real SATs. Still the PSAT score was the first hard number we'd have, the first milestone (for us at least) in the long march, and without much effort I had worked myself into considerable anxiety about how he'd done—an anxiety that *The Truth About Getting In* had done an excellent job of worsening. With my customary agility, against the rocking of the train, I tapped out a text message to my son—*anyp sa t sores yet?*—and pressed send. (I don't bother to correct the typos because I don't know how.) When the train rolled into Connecticut, after dark, I still hadn't heard from him.

ROD, COHEN'S ASSISTANT, WAS WAITING for me by the platform. He was snappily dressed in a three-button suit and bright red tie, and very friendly. When I asked after "Dr. Cohen," he waved a hand.

"Kat," he said. "Everybody calls her Kat. Once you meet her, you never think of calling her Dr. Cohen. She's just Kat."

Kat had hired Rod from Columbia University, where he'd worked in admissions. Most of Kat's employees come directly from the admissions office of similarly fancy schools.

"She hires young people because she likes to keep it fresh," he told me. "But they have to have that real-world experience."

Kat's counselors, and of course Kat herself, were presumed to have an insider's familiarity with this deeply mysterious process. That's what Kat was selling: the kind of expertise that could only come from a professional who had helped make the process mysterious in the first place. I knew this approach from years writing about Congress. On Capitol Hill they call it the revolving door. Young committee staffers draft legislation that places a tangle of elaborate and confusing legal burdens on large corporations, who then have to hire the staffers to find loopholes in the legislation they helped draft.

Rod walked me through the security desks in the bank lobby. After hours it was mostly empty. We caught an elevator to the top floor, where the doors slid open into a Versailles-like conference room. Glass windows two stories high looked out into the darkness and onto the sparkling Connecticut suburbs below. On the walls opposite were paintings by Michael Mazur, each of them covering an area the size of an upended tennis court. The carpet was so thickly woven you could bounce on it. The place reeked of cash, and so, of course, did the invitation-only gathering of well-to-do parents. A significant majority of them, I noticed, were women, dressed in Greenwich casual, suggesting that they were stay-at-home-in-Fairfield-County moms, who are distinguished from ordinary stay-at-home moms by not resembling moms. Not moms with college-age kids, anyway. They wore tight designer jeans and complicated shoes with spiked heels. Nearly everyone was blond. The emphatic cheekbones and jawlines looked as if they could have been sculpted from Carrara marble, if Carrara marble were the color of Permatan.

A lady from the bank told us to take our seats. Thirty or forty chairs had been set out, with an aisle running down the middle. We sat down so she could start scaring us.

"Let's say you've got three kids," the bank lady said. I looked around. It was highly unlikely that anyone here had birthed more than two, which is regulation for the American upper middle class. But nobody blanched. "They're in grade school, kindergarten, pre-K. You want them to go to college somewhere close to home, here in Connecticut. One goes to Yale, one to UConn, one to Fairfield. How much will tuition cost you when they start applying fifteen years from now? For all three. Anybody?"

A few people took a stab at it, highballing the answer, the way you should when a speaker makes it clear she wants to shock you with a larger-than-expected sum. Five hundred thousand? one woman called out. Huh-uh. Six? Wrong. Seven-fifty?

"Nine hundred and fifty thousand dollars," she said triumphantly. "At a minimum. Could be more."

A number at the edge of seven figures had apparently occurred to no one. A million bucks to send your kids to college? She had our attention. It turned out she was a financial adviser, and this stratospheric number was meant to force us into confronting the challenge of college admissions—by, just for example, investing more of our money with her bank. The gambit wasn't really necessary, though. Everyone in the room was on full alert, with that feral look of parental ambition. They swiveled their tail-gunning eyes toward Kat when she was introduced.

She was tiny. But the glamour in the book jacket photo wasn't a Photoshop trick. She was dressed all in black: flared slacks and a tight buttoned-down shirt, topped with a string of pearls, and hoisted on a pair of high heels with that pointy toe that appeals to women and frightens men. With long painted nails she adjusted the microphone clipped to her collar and began strolling up the aisle.

She was the second swing of a one-two punch. The financial adviser made us wonder how we'd pay for college, Kat made us worry how our kids would get in, even if we could pay.

"How many people have kids they want to see get into a selective college?" she asked. She cast her eyes across the forest of upraised hands. "Everybody."

But what's a selective college? Harvard, with an acceptance rate well under 10 percent, isn't the most selective college in the United

17

States, she said. Neither is Yale, also with an acceptance below 10 percent.

"The most selective schools in America are Juilliard and Curtis," she said, referring to the two arts conservatories. "But look here." She waved a card with more numbers on it. "The acceptance rate at Flagler College is twenty-six percent. City University of New York, it's twenty percent. Brigham Young University Hawaii? Nineteen percent. College of the Ozarks has a twelve percent acceptance rate."

She let the numbers sink in, and you could almost feel the shudder run through these East Coast moms: my kid won't be able to get into *College of the Ozarks*? What the f . . . and wait a minute—where's Flagler College?

Kat said she wanted us to learn how to think like an admissions officer. Admissions committees at selective schools call their method "holistic," which involves weighing a dozen intangible factors along with hard data like SAT scores and grade-point averages in deciding whom to admit. The word "holistic" is meant to distinguish their method from the purely numerical process at less-selective state universities or community colleges, where a committee will automatically admit any applicant with scores or grades above an explicit threshold. It's a cagey word, "holistic," borrowed from New Age yogis, Gestalt therapists, makers of herbal toothpaste, and other mystifiers whose prestige depends on your not being able to figure out exactly what they're doing. A more practical and accurate term for holistic admissions is "completely subjective."

Kat handed out photocopied sheets that summarized the résumés of four college applicants—grades, test scores, extracurricular activities, recommendations, summer activities. The applicants' names had been changed but the résumés were real.

"You're going to be Jim Miller, the dean of admissions at Brown University," she said. Oh, Brown—a couple in the row ahead of me glanced at each other at the mention of the name. Small, old, New Englandish, ivy-covered, Brown casts a spell over many parents.

Kat herself had worked in the admissions office there. She told us that the typical admissions officer spends an average of five minutes reading an application, so tonight she'd give us ten to look over these—after which we'd get to choose who we'd admit to that little slice of higher-ed heaven in Providence, Rhode Island. ("Heaven in Providence, Rhode Island" . . . some phrases you never think you'll type, and then . . .)

I looked through the résumés. Joe, Reggie, Kim, and Teresa were all SuperKids. Of course. More SuperKids. Dress them in capes and tights and they could star in their own comic book. Joe had an 800 SAT in math and raised money for a Native American school. Reggie had six Advanced Placement classes and a 4.0 grade-point average. Kim was a fiddle player who had recorded her own violin concertos with the local symphony orchestra. Teresa single-handedly kept a nearby Hispanic grade school afloat while acing her SATs. Where do these people come from? Mentally, and invidiously, I flipped through my son's résumé. I had to do this mentally because his résumé didn't exist. It had never occurred to any of us to put such a thing together.

After ten minutes we cast votes—Teresa won and got admitted to heaven—but Kat made clear that our own preferences weren't the point of the exercise. At Brown the admit rate is 14 percent, she said. A school like Brown receives thousands of applications from superior students. In most important respects, on paper, they are indistinguishable from one another.

"There are thirty-six thousand high schools in this country," she said. "That means there are at least thirty-six thousand valedictorians. They can't all go to Brown. You could take the 'deny pile' of applications and make two more classes that were every bit as solid as the class that gets in."

The challenge for admissions officers at highly selective schools is therefore to find reasons *not* to admit an applicant. It followed that for the parent of an applicant the challenge was not to give them a reason to say no.

Yet the reasons were so easy to find! In the seemingly flaw-less credentials of these SuperKids she picked up one disqualify-ing imperfection after another, speaking of them as though they wiggled at the tip of a forceps.

"Look at Joe," she said. "He has the highest class rank of any of them. That's good, right? Look closer. No AP classes!" AP classes are the rigorous courses that high schools often provide for brighter students. "This is an important lesson: it is always better to take a more rigorous course load with lots of APs and get a lower GPA than to have a 4.0 with a light course load and no APs." Exit Joe.

She turned her attention to Kim's résumé.

"Now, Kim. Her class rank—not so great. Top twenty percent. The grades are only okay until junior year. Then she shows a big improvement. But it might be too little too late. You question her seriousness. Did she just discover her potential during her junior year because she suddenly got worried about college?

"The violin concertos and the symphony are impressive. But see here under her ECs"—extracurricular activities—"it says, 'She does not participate in school orchestra.' It's all about her. Colleges are looking for someone who will contribute to their school com-munities, who will enrich the experience of the whole school. Kim may be passionate about her music, but she's not giving back to her school."

It was like a scolding, almost—worse, actually. Kim's applica-tion essay was about returning to her parents' ancestral homeland. So hackneyed. Kat said Kim seemed to be eerily single-minded. Maybe a bit freakish. By the time Kat was through with her, Kim's body lay limp and bloody on the floor, the fiddle snapped in two beside her.

Kat moved up and down the aisle like a drill sergeant. She brought Joe back for a stomping. His fund-raiser for the Native American school was just a "one-shot deal, right at the end of junior year." No commitment again. And the timing is pretty sus-picious. "He's just piling it on for the application." For his summer activity before his junior year Joe had earned a scholarship to a four-week scuba-diving camp.

"What did he do the other six or eight weeks that summer? There's nothing here to tell us."

One of the mothers objected. "We paid four thousand dollars for a four-week scuba class for our son," she said, sounding slightly offended.

Kat stopped in her tracks and gave her a blank look.

"You did?" she said.

"Yes," the mother said.

"Then I feel sorry for you."

The mom's voice rose and Kat interrupted. "Look, look," she said. "I'm not saying it's *bad*. I'm just saying it won't make a difference. Not if your son wants to go to this college. It just won't."

She moved on to Reggie. He took six AP classes. It sounded like a lot to me. (I made a note: How many APs is my son taking?) But at the prestigious boarding school Reggie goes to, Kat said, kids typically take eight to ten AP classes. So Reggie's mere six suggest a slacker. But look here: under his extracurriculars Reggie listed no fewer than twelve activities: model UN, chess club, drama club, and so on. Busy kid!

Kat wasn't buying it. She just shook her head.

"He's a serial joiner," she said. "There are a lot of 'one hour a week' type things. In the end they don't add up to anything. There's no commitment—no *depth* of commitment. It's like he's just running up the score."

None of the parents had the nerve to object that the reverse could as easily be true. A kid who had only a single extracurricular to which he was intensely committed could be rejected by an admissions dean because he showed no diversity of interests, no sense of adventure—on account of monomania, maybe. I think it was beginning to dawn on us that the kids could be damned one way or the other, depending on the school, on the composition of the committee reviewing the application, even on the disposition of an individual member of the committee. A tough cookie like Kat could reject anybody. Even SuperKids were vulnerable, if only because there were so many of them. The most that helpless parents and applicants could do was to attend to what Kat called the "soft factors"—those bits of the résumé that lie at the margins, beyond the hard data of grades, class rank, course load, and SAT scores.

"These are the little things that might be the deal makers," she said.

There were those summer activities, for example. How kids spend their summers from middle school onward would tell an admissions dean a lot about their character, ambitions, commitment. Working at a job was fine, Kat said—but starting their own business would be better. If they didn't do that, then it made a difference where they worked. And avoid the last refuge of a slacker, lifeguarding.

My son had worked as a lifeguard the last two summers and was planning on doing it again.

Summer camp was out, Kat continued, even if you were working as a counselor: "Colleges are not going to be impressed with how many years' experience you've got playing spin the bottle." Family trips to Europe would serve only to draw attention to the kid's life of privilege. She was particularly dismissive of "leadership programs" that—for a fee—brought high schoolers to Washington, D.C., or the state capital for weeks of interning and seminars.

"But that's what my son did!"

Another mom was objecting.

"He was *invited* to do this," she said. "He got so much out of it, learning leadership skills."

"The invitation came in the mail, I guess," Kat said. "It said he was 'selected.' Do you know why he was selected? Your zip code. Because of your zip code, they knew you could pay." She shrugged. "Sorry."

"He was planning to write his application essay about it," the mom said, crestfallen.

About those essays, Kat went on: they could be beautifully written, tightly argued, evocative of time and place, but unless they showed something about the applicant that the résumé didn't—some passion, some struggle, some character-defining event that wasn't included in the list of extracurriculars and summer activities—then the essays were a wasted opportunity and utterly without effect. Community service had to be carefully chosen as well. It should be long-standing and, again, passionate; growing from a deep-seated interest of the kids themselves. Teacher recommendations, another soft factor, should be tended with similar care.

"Early on in high school your child should find a teacher they like and go that extra mile," she said. "They should spend time with that teacher, cultivate that relationship. Let that teacher know what they're interested in. They should be enthusiastic in class, add to the discussion, speak up—help the teacher make that classroom an exciting place. Each and every day they should ask themselves, 'How am I contributing to this class?' And spend time outside of class with the teacher, if that's possible."

And then, when the applications are due and you need a letter of recommendation, the pump will be primed to release a gusher of praise.

I was new to this, but already I saw I had got it all wrong. At its most intense, the admissions process didn't force kids to be Lisa Simpson; it turned them into Eddie Haskell. ("You look lovely in that new dress, Ms. Admissions Counselor.") It guaranteed that teenagers would pursue life with a single ulterior motive, while pretending they weren't. It coated their every undertaking in a thin lacquer of insincerity. Befriending people in hopes of a good rec letter; serving the community to advertise your big heart; studying hard just to puff up the GPA and climb the greasy poll of class rank—nothing was done for its own sake. Do good; do well; but make sure you can prove it on a college app.

So the first great task consuming our children as they step into the wider world is an act of marketing, with themselves as a product.

If this bothered any of the other parents I didn't hear about it. They matter-of-factly accepted the idea, with the additional consideration that, like professional marketers, they and their kids might have to hire an outside consultant. After the meeting broke up, Kat disappeared in a scrum of parents who reached for her business card and tried to squeeze out more bits of free advice. The stack of free copies of *The Truth About Getting In* vanished quickly. Trays of melon and grapes and squares of cheese had been laid out but went untouched by everyone except me. It was after my supper time.

"It's so complicated!"

One of the moms was suddenly next to me.

"Ir wully ib," I said through a bolus of Gouda.

"There's so much to do. My God. You hear stories, but I had no idea . . ."

I swallowed and asked her if she was thinking of hiring Kat's firm for help.

"I don't think we have a choice, do you?" She scanned the grapes without interest. "You've got to do *something*—if your kid's going to go somewhere we—she—can be proud of." I got the idea that "she" really did mean "we," which really meant "I."

Once the crowd was gone and Kat was free, we walked with Rod to the station to catch the late train back to Manhattan. I mentioned that the whole admissions process seemed to me like a giant self-marketing scheme. I wasn't sure my son had the personality for it.

"A shy person is going to be at a disadvantage in this process," she said. "It's a people process. It's not okay to be timid. You've got to be self-advocating. And it's very hard for some kids to do, especially at this age. That's one reason it's so important to start early!"

Of all the myths about admissions, she said, two of the most damaging involved the early start.

"People say, 'Ninth grade doesn't count—grades, ECs, they don't matter that early.' Yes they do! People say, 'It's okay to start junior year.' No it's not!"

By the time they were juniors, she said, students should be well on the way to putting together a compelling application. "Your application needs to scream, 'I want to go to this school!'"

I said my son wasn't a screamer. Worse, I didn't think there were any schools that he was just dying to go to.

"What year?" she said.

"He's a junior."

"And you're how far along?"

"Well," I said, "I'll put it this way. We didn't start in ninth grade. Or tenth."

"How many schools have you visited?"

"None," I said.

"Do you have a list?" Rod interjected. "Has he done any research at all?"

"No," I said.

"SAT prep?" Kat was smiling now.

I shook my head.

"Oooooh," she said. "Baaaaaaad daaaaaad."

I SPENT THE NIGHT IN New York. When I got up the next morning I saw my son had finally answered my text message. He'd gotten his PSAT scores and they were . . . good. At least I thought they were good. In the lobby of the hotel I logged on to a computer in the business center and went clicking through, trying to figure out what percentile the boy's raw numbers put him in. The percentile was . . . good. Slightly better than good. Not great. But still. I felt hugely relieved.

It wasn't more than a minute before I felt kind of disgusted with myself for feeling hugely relieved.

I made a vow: this would stop here. If what I had seen the night before—the feral looks, the anxiety, the unloosed competitive instincts—constituted a "good dad," I'd go ahead and be baaaaaaad. I would not confuse my own preferences with his interests. I would not entangle my own vanity with his performance. What was important was his future happiness, and the depth of learning that he could acquire, and the foundation he could lay for a worthy life. And none of those, I knew, was intrinsically tied to a particular college. Wherever he was admitted—wherever he chose to go—he could start from there, with the love and encouragement of his parents (plus money). I would, in short, back off.

KAT HAD AGREED TO MEET me for breakfast. She seemed slightly jittery. It turned out she had found herself in the same situation as her clients: she was trying to get her daughter into a prestigious school.

"We've got the application essay to worry about," she said. "And next week is the interview. There are tests to take too."

"So now you see what it feels like," I said.

"Exactly."

Well, not *exactly* exactly. Kat's daughter was nine months old. She was trying to get her into an exclusive day care in Manhattan. Applicants had to write an essay extolling their bright, passionate, emotionally mature, and worldly-but-idealistic infants and then sit for a home interview with a nosy instructor from the school, who arrived with a battery of baby tests to administer as well. The stakes were high: this day-care center fed into equally exclusive pre-Ks, which fed into prestigious kindergartens, which fed into even more exclusive grade schools, and then prep schools, and then, perhaps, eighteen years from now, the kid would be in a position to be crowned with admission to Princeton or Wellesley or Brown. One misstep at the beginning could doom the whole process.

"It's crazy," I said, when we had found a table. "How did we get here? How did all this get started?"

"All what get started?"

There wasn't a trace of cynicism in Kat. She had spent most of her professional life in this world of high competition, where children quite often served as proxies for status and parental self-worth, and she took the world as she found it. She ignored my question.

"Your son's PSATs," she said. "Did you hear?"

"They were pretty good," I said. "Not great. Good, though."

"Score?"

I told her, after I bumped the number up by 10 percent.

I was violating my vow already.

2

RANKINGS UP AND DOWN

A summer job—Hasselhoff's bad example—
an unhelpful meeting—the painted chest—
a simple history of a complicated subject—
confusion in the chaos
the most powerful man in the world—
a newsmagazine spots a trend—inputs and outcomes—
outrage from Yale—
Washington U. and Clemson climb the page—
an unwelcome gift

"WHAT'S WRONG with lifeguarding?" my son asked.

"I just think you could find something more substantial," I said. "Volunteer work, maybe."

"I need the money," he said. And he liked a lifeguard's hours. He liked the routine. He liked the people he worked with.

Which is another thing: nearly all the people he worked with at the pool were from Eastern Europe—interesting people and good company and, I gathered, reliable coworkers. Lifeguarding was once a standard means of keeping the American teenager occupied and gainfully employed for a summer. Now we were importing our lifeguards from faraway lands. The reason was the obsession with college—you never knew where its effects were going to turn up.

Native-born high school kids, my son's peers, were getting internships at investment banks and brokerage houses and advertising agencies, maybe even starting businesses, as Kat said. They were already laying pipe for their subsequent careers and, more immediately, for their college applications. Lifeguarding was not a life goal; nobody's going to make a career as a professional lifeguard, with all respect to David Hasselhoff. And childhood now was a matter of setting life goals and arranging your activities in pursuit of them. So my son's peers were doing the smart thing: Why lifeguard when you can be loading up the brag sheet?

"Or you could start your own business," I said.

He looked skyward. He was not, I knew, the entrepreneurial type, and that was fine with me. The literature often refers to the college application phase of life as a kind of therapy—a "journey," to use the unavoidable phrase, or worse, a "process of personal growth," propelled by introspection and self-discovery. I was wary of this talk of transformation. My son was highly satisfactory the way he was. A good student, motivated, kind, honest so far as I could tell, he didn't seem to me to be in need of a prolonged program in character development, even if it was barely disguised as applying to colleges. I did, however, want him to get serious about applying to the damn colleges. The character development I could take or leave.

MY WIFE AND I HAD joined him at his high school to meet with his college counselor for the first time. The initial consultation was a big item on every checklist, and, as Kat had pointed out with considerable force, we were behind schedule. The counselor was a dour and distracted man who showed little obvious interest in college or higher education of any kind, particularly as it pertained to my son.

He opened the meeting with pro forma questions: What kind of school do you want to go to? Big school, small school, state school, private school?

"Big," the boy said. "I'd like something with a good sports pro-gram. Division One. Someplace that people have heard of."

The counselor jotted on a pad. As they spoke I realized that for all my fretting, I had never had this conversation with my son. I was learning these things—like what kind of school he wanted to go to—for the first time. *Baaaaaaad . . .*

It emerged that my son's preferences were unformed. He wasn't sure about a course of study—"not science," he said, "and not math"—and he was indifferent to the school's location, so long as the winters weren't punishingly cold.

"Good," said the counselor. He looked up from his pad. He mentioned various realistic options. Some big private schools like Notre Dame or University of Pennsylvania might be a stretch, but others, like Wake Forest or Tufts, were within reach; maybe USC, with some luck. All of these were quite expensive, he noted, shoot-ing a glance at me and my wife, though financial aid of various kinds was usually available and might provide considerable relief. There were also state schools nearby—Ohio or Indiana, which was my wife's alma mater—that would be more affordable than the pri-vate schools. And our own state had several public schools of vari-ous sizes that would be much less expensive even than these. There were a couple of state-run small liberal arts colleges, and Tech, an enormous school in a far corner of the state that specialized in architecture, engineering, and hard sciences. There was even a state military school (*"No,"* my son said hurriedly). The flagship was Big State University. It was the oldest public school in the state, tucked in an idyllic college town about two hours away. BSU had major-conference sports teams that showed up on ESPN, where the rest of the country could enjoy their routine humiliation.

Of these, my son particularly liked Notre Dame, Wake For-est, and BSU, also Boston College, and USC, a distant dream. He said he'd like to apply to a few other out-of-state schools—Indiana at least, and North Carolina. Aside from the military school he showed strong feeling only in a single instance, by expressing contempt for Penn. His disdain ran to the entire state of Pennsylvania, not merely to its most prestigious university. I glimpsed the logic of his decision making when I learned that the revulsion had its origins in a disastrous family weekend we'd once spent in Philadelphia, reinforced by a more rational dislike of the Phillies and their loudmouthed fans.

The counselor said we could come up with other possibilities as the process wore on. And a college tour, he added, would help my son hone his idea of the kind of school he'd like.

The reach and variety of American higher education, even including the schools we could almost afford, seemed suddenly limitless. There was something for every taste. It was like picking out a mattress at a discount warehouse, without the discount.

"I can tell you the kind of school I'd really like," my son told the college counselor, with an air of finality. "I want to go to a place where I can go to a football game, take off my shirt, paint my chest, and major in beer."

WE WERE OUT IN THE parking lot.

"Did you see his face?" I said to my son, annoyed.

"He was smiling," he said.

"He was wincing."

"No, he thought it was funny. Didn't he?"

"Does he know you?"

"Sure. Kind of. Not really."

"Well, he probably thinks he knows you now," I said. "He probably wrote it down on his pad: 'Ferguson. Smart-ass.' It'll be a big help when he writes your recommendation."

"I was kidding."

"Are you sure?"

"Kind of," he said.

I WAS STILL CAUGHT UP in the question that I'd asked Kat at breakfast and that she seemed uninterested in answering: "How did we get here? How did this all get started? Where do the craziness and excess come from?"

The answers are harder to find than I would have thought. The history of American higher education has attracted comparatively little interest among academics. It probably looks to them like a busman's holiday, writing about the job. Only a few popular histories have been written that qualify as comprehensive, and each of these is largely devoted to refuting the others. The classic work was written in the early 1960s by Frederick Rudolph, a historian at Williams College, who relied heavily on official campus histories produced by the most well-established schools. As witty and readable as it is, the book imposes an artificial tidiness on its subject, as later histories revealed. The development of American colleges and universities, like the development of business and religion, wasn't methodical or linear. It was purely American: noisy, makeshift, entrepreneurial, competitive, going off in a dozen directions at once.

In their formative years American colleges often aped the organizational plan of their European forerunners, whether the segmented and stratified German model or the less formal but equally hierarchical British version. The Old World imprint is felt in many of the customs we take for granted, such as tenure, academic freedom, the departmental system, faculty research, and the nine-month school calendar. What is purely American is the mind-boggling variety, the riot of styles and purposes that our system allows for.

The variety was there from the start. The first schools of higher education were founded by rival Protestant denominations to train their own divines. Yale, for example, was founded as an orthodox alternative to the permissiveness of Harvard. (Now they're both permissive.) The snooty Anglicans built the College of William and Mary. Princeton was founded by "New Light" Presbyterians trying to unshackle themselves from their "Old Light" adversaries. All of these sects were united in their desire to snub the Congregationalists, who founded Dartmouth in retaliation. Brown University was brought into the world by Old School Baptists, an especially strict group of believers who these days must look down upon Providence, Rhode Island, from Baptist heaven, wondering what they did wrong.

As American religion exfoliated through the nineteenth century, so did higher education. The growth was greatly aided by the decentralized nature of American government. Despite occasional efforts to establish one, the country had no national university, nor would it ever, since those who considered the idea an affront to federalism and local sovereignty have carried the day. Instead every region and commonwealth wanted its own college, and sometimes two. It was a point of pride and proof of cultural refinement. State charters and even public funding were easy to come by. This opened the field to what the sociologist Randall Collins called "educational entrepreneurs"—academic wildcatters "who traveled the country from college to college, often founding and abandoning" several colleges over the span of a few years. In his book, Frederick Rudolph estimates that by the time of the Civil War one thousand colleges had been founded in the United States—far more, in proportion to the population, than any country had ever seen. And of those thousand, nearly seven hundred had gone bust.

College wasn't an ivory-tower enterprise, in other words: the boom-and-bust cycles that hit American industry and agriculture roiled the schools too. Supply would increase until it outstripped demand, after which supply would be culled and schools would close their doors, some of them to reopen when demand revived. But equilibrium has been elusive. Most historians seem to think that supply has always exceeded demand in American higher education. In 1862, Congress passed the Morrill Act, ceding federal lands to the states for the building of "land-grant colleges." The purpose, Senator Justin Smith Morrill said, was to make good on the democratic ideal. His bill would "promote the liberal and practical education of the industrial classes in the several pursuits and professions of life." Each school was to have an agricultural division too. The bill passed over the objections of senators who fretted that it might make the common folk uppity. "We want no fancy farmers," one senator pleaded. "We want no fancy mechanics."

The spirit of democratic idealism was still alive eighty years later, in the GI Bill, which guaranteed a college education for veterans of World War II. At tremendous expense, both the Morrill Act and the GI Bill drew on a principle that could fly only in a country like this: everyone who wants the chance to go to college should have it. Mechanics could be as fancy as they wanted to be; and if they didn't want to be mechanics at all, they could find a way out, through higher education. A decade after the Morrill Act became law, slightly less than 2 percent of Americans between the ages of eighteen and twenty-one were in college. Today the figure is more than 60 percent.

By the lights of old Europe the notion of mass higher education is preposterous. There the traditional method for selecting students worthy of college education was most often a rigorous system of exams. The results could be used to shunt students into university or away from it, into the proper occupational slots where they would beaver away for life; very orderly, very rational. In the traditional view, the American alternative would bring chaos.

Which it did.

IN AMERICA STUDENTS WENT OFF to college with multiple and often contradictory expectations. But one expectation was shared above all others: higher ed should be useful. It should prove its value in dollars and cents. In American higher education democratic idealism met economic pragmatism. In the last fifty years a college degree became what it had never been before: the necessary credential for the most desirable jobs in the market, especially in professions that had once been taught in less-formal apprenticeships, such as law and medicine. Social ambition entered in as well; never underestimate the pull of snobbery. On its own a college degree could no longer be enough to satisfy the craving for status. If "everyone" was going to school, then it mattered very much what schools everyone was going to. Thus the many Americans who for the first time were able to enjoy the blessings of higher education—racial and ethnic minorities, the lower middle class—were also able to share in an experience that, in earlier times, had been denied to all but the lucky few: grinding anxiety about finding a college that reflected well on their kids, and on them.

With the arrival of the baby boom—the children of those veterans who had benefited from the GI Bill—colleges and universities thrived. They took in more money than ever before, spent more, and expanded beyond their most fervid dreams. But they hadn't escaped the cycle of boom and bust. In the early 1970s the most alert college administrators gazed a few years into the future and saw disaster looming. When the last of the boomers graduated, the number of college-age kids would go into steep decline. Faced with a dwindling number of customers who could fill those newly enlarged dorms and classroom buildings, colleges and universities reacted like any other industry: they groveled, they pandered, they seized every technique of modern marketing to draw attention to themselves and away from the competition.

By the time the decline reversed itself, the nature of college admissions had been transformed. For Americans who had gone to college in the fifties, sixties, or early seventies, a process that had seemed rather straightforward—find a school, preferably nearby, figure out how to pay for it, leave home, study, flirt, party—now appeared unexpectedly elaborate and crucially important, complicated by a bewildering array of plausible options and eager come-ons. Parents seemed slightly stunned, and then uneasy, and then confused.

And so we remained until one day in 1983, when the third most popular of the country's three weekly newsmagazines, *U.S. News & World Report,* arrived on newsstands with a new issue, promising to bring some order to the chaotic bazaar that American higher education had become. And then we got *really* confused.

I ONCE WENT OUT TO lunch with Bob Morse, who's overseen the *U.S. News* college rankings for more than twenty years. At a corner table sat George Will, the newspaper columnist and TV pundit, and a distant acquaintance. I introduced him to Bob.

"Bob is responsible for the *U.S. News* college rankings," I said.

"Aha," said Will, rising to his feet and making an ironical bow, "the most powerful man in America."

He doesn't look the part. Bob is a shy, unassuming man, small in stature, with a look of constant worry and the manner of someone who, if it's all the same to you, would really rather just go back to the office and scroll though a really good spreadsheet. He speaks softly and slowly, and most of his sentences come to rest in a long, consuming silence, sometimes before they've had a chance to finish. But Will's joke was only a slight exaggeration, and I've since met college administrative officers who wouldn't think it was an exaggeration at all. *U.S. News* didn't invent college rankings, but its brand is the most popular and far-reaching in influence, maintaining a long lead in sales and prominence over its many imitators, both in the United States and more than thirty other countries. And maintaining the brand is Bob Morse's life work.

College administrators often profess to hate the rankings. The president of USC has said they "bordered on fraud." Another college president once compared them to poison, others use words like "madness" and a "hoax." The president of Occidental College a few years ago called *U.S. News* rankings a "tyrannical tool," used to bully schools into conforming to a distasteful commercial standard—"superficial," "misleading," and "destructive of educational values." Wherever admissions deans gather, the hallways ring with condemnations of the magazine. Meanwhile, the same administrators read it, feed it, and fidget all summer until the new edition arrives, and then wave it around like a bride's garter belt if their school gets a favorable review.

This conflicted reaction is not unusual among higher-ed professionals. They often participate in undertakings that, according to them, are destructive of their most earnest ideals—not just the college rankings but also standardized tests, along with direct-mail campaigns, cut-rate pricing, blast e-mails, consumer research, and many other grungy techniques of American commercialism. A lot of these guys, they're tortured souls.

THE *U.S. NEWS* GUIDE ACQUIRED its power because, by design or dumb luck, it has perfectly reflected the shifting views that Americans themselves have held about college. As higher education was democratized, a college degree became more desirable than the learning it was originally meant to signify. It was a guarantor of smarts, drive, social standing, and future prospects. As the historian David F. Labaree put it, "What matters most is not the knowledge [students] attain in school but the credentials they acquire there." We didn't care if we ate the dinner as long as we could take home the menu, to prove to our neighbors that we'd been to a fancy restaurant.

U.S. News was the first college guide to absorb this reality. Earlier college guides—there were only a few of them, and they were of interest mostly to academics—had assessed a school on the basis of its product, that is, on the graduates it produced and how much they knew, how much they went on to accomplish in the wider world. In Edwardian England one gung-ho guide to universities was called *Where We Get Our Best Men.* Here in the States a college guide in the 1930s judged schools on how many alumni were listed in *Who's Who in America.*

Methods like these would be unconvincing in the country as

it exists today. Now that we know a person can buy his way into it, the agate-type blowhards and self-promoters in *Who's Who* are much less impressive than they used to be. And our fractured public could never agree on who "Our Best Men (or Persons)" were. The genius of the *U.S. News* guide, in its earliest incarnation, was to find a way around this impasse. The editors decided to base their assessments not on a school's product but on its reputation—not on the kind of people it graduated but on the kind of things people were saying about it. The rankings would be *reputational*.

No one at the magazine recalls any longer who first came up with the idea for a college guide. For several years, *U.S. News* had surveyed important Americans to compile an annual list of important Americans. It was a gimmick—and a circular and incestuous one at that, since it gave big shots a license to guard their big-shot reputation by naming one another and keeping it all in the family. Newsmagazines used to thrive on off-the-shelf stunts like this; it offered them a cover story that almost wrote itself once a year and it moved units. For the same reason, newsmagazines were always inventing bogus trends. "America's New Homebodies: Why More Nannies Are Playing Chess." "Liposuction Nation: The Fad That's Sweeping America—and Your Tummy's Next!" It didn't matter if the trends were phantoms of an editor's imagination. Indeed, that was one point in their favor: the more unlikely the trend, the less chance a rival newsweekly would beat you to putting it on the cover. The "Most Influential Americans" issue was always a signature success for *U.S. News*. The notion that a magazine could rank the fifty people who exert more control over national events than the next fifty people was so transparently absurd, it took years for the other two newsmagazines to start doing it too.

Many of the magazine's most influential Americans, and many of the influential Americans who were asked to identify the most influential Americans, were college presidents. Why not, while they were at it, ask them to identify the best colleges, assign each college a rank, and then publish the results? So that's what the editors did. And they stumbled upon the Holy Grail of newsweekly journalism: a *real* trend. Several trends, in fact, all of them real and all of them taking off at once.

UNIVERSAL HIGHER ED BECAME A plausible ideal just as the cost of tuition began its stratospheric rise. (The two developments are most likely related, as I learned later.) Even aside from simple status anxiety, Americans who had never before considered college for themselves or their children suddenly had fresh practicalities to agonize about: where would they go, how would they pay for it, and how would they know they were getting their money's worth? The astonishing eruption of wealth in postwar America created the world's first "consumer society," and in a society where the consumer is king everything will sooner or later be considered a commodity. Why not a college education? Once the value of higher ed shifted from that hard-to-define abstraction *learning* to the much more concrete *credential,* it was easier to think of college admissions as an item to shop for. And if it had a price tag, it needed a consumer guide.

The editors failed at first to understand what they'd fallen into. The debut issue came out in 1983, the next one two years later, and not till two years after that did they see that the "Best Colleges" issue could become an annual money machine. State Farm Insurance was signed up as lead sponsor and advertiser. Timed to coincide with the beginning of the school year, the special issue annually gave birth to a thick book, *U.S. News America's Best Colleges,* which could stay on newsstands year round, ready to be plucked by a parent's trembling hand and taken home whenever the spirit demanded.

The reputational methodology made the list easy to assemble. Roughly two hundred colleges and universities were sorted by region, size, and mission. The survey asked 1,300 college presidents to name the top ten schools in their category. The rest was simple addition. The guide listed the top twenty-five vote getters for each type of school. (I'm relying heavily here on a brief history of the rankings written a few years ago by the late Alvin Sanoff, a long-time *U.S. News* editor.)

The first book-size guide sold more than a million copies. Alarmed, college presidents went public with their objections to the *U.S. News* "beauty contest." More than forty signed a letter to the editors demanding the magazine "cease and desist." There was some justice in their complaint. The reputational survey was superficial and unfair, they said, because a college president was qualified to judge only his own school—leaving the more important corollary unstated, that only a college president was qualified to judge his own school. And the rankings' self-reinforcing circularity was as obvious as it had been when those influential Americans were listing the most influential Americans. The famous schools would come out on top simply because they were famous, thus making them more famous and more likely to come out on top next time.

Sanoff writes that the editors knew the guide would never be taken seriously as a journalistic enterprise—or enjoy staying power as a commercial proposition—unless they revised their methods. In January 1988 they held a come-to-Jesus meeting in the *U.S. News* offices with the forty school presidents. The editors agreed to toughen up the magazine's methodology. The results of the reputational survey would account for only 25 percent of a school's rank. The rest would be data. The average SAT scores and the high school class rank of incoming freshmen would give an idea of the kind of kids the school attracted. The acceptance rate would show selectivity or the lack of it. The "yield," the percentage of students who are accepted and then decide to enroll, would also suggest the degree of selectivity. The student–faculty ratio, average class size, and expenditures per student might suggest the quality of the student's classroom experience. Faculty salary and the number of tenured PhDs would give a sense of the quality of teaching. And the rate of alumni donations, the graduation rate, and the percentage of freshmen who returned for their sophomore year might serve as a measure of how happy students were with the school—a measure, that is, of consumer satisfaction.

Much of this data was furnished to *U.S. News* by the schools themselves. Before the rankings appeared, a consumer had no way of acquiring this information and comparing it across schools—a convenience that we've taken for granted ever since. In the *U.S. News* offices, however, the editors were drowning in data. There were numbers, numbers everywhere. They needed someone to tease meaning from the figures and arrange the results in an accessible presentation. They needed an ace statistician. They needed Bob Morse, and they found him right down the hall.

BOB INVITED ME TO MEET him at his office so I could see where the world's preeminent college guide and rankings are knit together. I used to drop by the *U.S. News* offices in the late 1980s, to visit friends who worked there. Back then the editorial staff spread across several bustling floors of an impressive office building in a gentrified neighborhood at the fringe of downtown Washington. The magazine had a smaller circulation than *Time* or *Newsweek*, and the reach of its reporting wasn't quite so long as theirs, but it was still immensely profitable and had acquired a loyal readership of more than a million subscribers. Unfortunately for the business model, most of those million subscribers were about to die of old age.

It was a different century, when newsweeklies were pashas of the magazine trade. The offices have moved a few times since, and when Bob came out to greet me in the foyer I saw that the old bustle is gone. A magazine rack stamped with the *U.S. News* logo stood on a table, empty. Leading away from the entrance was a kind of memorial wall, hung with poster-size black-and-white photos of bygone editors in rumpled suits and ties askew, all of them smoking, huddled around a conference table to interview some long forgotten Great Man. And beyond that, down the hall, were cubicles for editors and writers, also empty, arranged in rows like cenotaphs. *U.S. News & World Report* is no longer published weekly. After heavy layoffs, the print magazine comes out once a month, but nobody in Washington seems quite sure when. Most of the editorial activity has moved to the magazine's Web site. The offices themselves are a kind of death notice for print journalism.

Only the national obsession with college keeps the old carcass breathing. The usual joke is that *U.S. News* is now a college guide with a newsmagazine attached. The gag is a bit out-of-date, for the rankings, published as *America's Best Colleges,* have now been joined by the *Ultimate Guide to Medical Schools, America's Best Graduate Schools,* the *Ultimate Guide to Law Schools, America's Best Boarding Schools,* the *World's Best Colleges and Universities,* and *America's Best High Schools,* all appearing under the *U.S. News* brand. The editors, including Bob, complain that outsiders exaggerate the profits that the special issues and college guides bring in, but they don't deny the magazine would be broke without them. It's a can't-miss moneymaker. Staff overhead is small—it's just Bob, a couple of tech geeks, a copy editor or two, and writers borrowed part-time from the regular magazine. Ad revenue from schools, test-prep programs, and financial services is high, and the magazine spends next to nothing on marketing, since each year's arrival is heralded by news stories and a blast of press releases from colleges and universities. Best of all, each summer brings a fresh audience, as last year's customers move on to college with a sigh of relief and the sophomores and juniors in high school move up to become juniors and seniors, hungry for help.

Since 1989, the formula that determines the rankings has been periodically adjusted. Indicators are assigned more weight or less, while new components have been added and others dropped, through trial and error and in response to criticism, which is continuous. It arrives from administrators, professors, and education activists, in studies, broadsides, and newspaper op-eds. Bob regularly convenes a panel of statisticians and college professionals to assess his methodology. Even so, it's hard to think of a problem in American higher education, from inequality to bureaucratic bloat, that has not been traced to the malign influence of Bob Morse and his rankings. The rankings are still just a beauty contest, the critics say, measuring a school's superficial attributes—its fame, wealth, and exclusivity. They create perverse incentives throughout higher education: schools ignore their educational mission and dedicate themselves to public relations, fund-raising, and attracting affluent kids with the highest scores and grades, merely to raise their rank— merely "to climb the page," as admissions people put it.

The criticisms boil down to the same gripe: Bob's formula relies too heavily on "inputs" rather than "outcomes," to use the jargon of social science. A school can win a high rank if it spends lavishly, builds big libraries, hires lots of faculty with PhDs, and enrolls freshmen with stratospheric SAT scores—all key indicators for Bob and *U.S. News.* But the rank won't answer the crucial questions an applicant should be asking. Are all those profs with PhDs good teachers? Do they teach at all, or do they turn their chores over to graduate students? Is anybody studying in those big libraries? And what's the lavish spending for, new chem labs or new hot tubs in the dorm? Are the graduates getting good jobs? *Is any learning going on around here?*

But this failing reflects our own. Parents crazed by college ambition are more concerned with getting their kids into a desirable school than with questioning why a school is considered desirable in the first place. It's the old story. We confuse a coveted degree with an excellent education—eat the menu instead of the dinner.

THE WEAKNESSES OF THE RANKINGS reflect another reality too, one that's no fault of *U.S. News.* There's lots of useful information about "outcomes" at American colleges and universities. But it's not public. It comes from the National Survey of Student Engagement (the acronym is pronounced "Nessie," like the monster in Scotland). Every year a nonprofit consortium surveys students at the request of individual schools; so far NSSE has gathered data on 1,200 colleges and universities, including most of the schools that everybody has heard of. Many of the questions get to the heart of how, or whether, learning happens at a college. Students report how much time they spend with professors, and what happens when they do. They report how many books they've had to read and papers they've had to write, and how professors allocate class time between lecture and discussion. Are tests and essays returned promptly? How much of a student's time out of class is spent studying? Is the work mostly memorization or does it require the manipulation of abstract ideas? Do students tend to study singly or in groups, and are they encouraged to do one or the other? Is help readily available from tutors?

According to the participating schools and NSSE statisticians, these are the factors that determine the quality of a higher education. For years *U.S. News* has asked participating schools to make the NSSE results public. Not only would the information be invaluable to the most energetic applicants and their parents; the rest of us, less driven to find it for ourselves, could see it immediately funneled into Bob Morse's formula and come out in the rankings. The effect might be revolutionary.

Which is probably why all but a handful of college presidents have decided to keep the NSSE results secret.

"The hypocrisy is endless," Bob says. Even with his customary reserve and politeness, he sounds bitter when he talks about college presidents. I can't blame him. For twenty years they have criticized the *U.S. News* rankings for lacking precision and authority—for obsessing about inputs when outcomes are what really matter— even as they sit on the outcomes data that might make the rankings more authoritative and precise.

"After a while you learn to expect it," he said. We were sitting in his office, in a fortress of paper: towers of yellowing reports and studies, battlements formed from spreadsheets, old guidebooks rising in ramparts along the wall. Peeking out from it all was a keyboard and computer screen, and as we spoke Bob went over to it often, hunching over the keyboard and with a few keystrokes producing some new bit of spreadsheet wizardry that he proudly displayed and that I tried, in vain, to understand. He was trained as an economist, and *U.S. News* first hired him to crunch numbers for a now-defunct "economics unit." His move to the college rankings full-time, in 1987, ensured that the endeavor would acquire statistical sophistication. He likes data—more than he likes words, I think—and is always trying to get more.

"We'd love to have the outcomes data," he said. "[But] we're left with the indicators we have. The truth is, even if we did have all that data, they still would complain. They still wouldn't like the rankings."

The "reputational survey" of college administrators remains the most heavily criticized indicator. In 2007 a dozen college presidents signed a letter calling for a boycott of the peer assessment, and the following year, for the first time, half of those surveyed declined to fill it out. Bob is undeterred. If the presidents and provosts won't participate in the reputational survey, he's got other professionals who will—high school counselors, for example, who make it their business to track the quality of colleges and universities. Like it or not, he said, reputation is important.

"A school's reputation helps you get a good job," he said. "It helps graduates get into graduate school. Reputation counts. The rankings should reflect that."

One reason for the staying power of *U.S. News* rankings has been Bob's doggedness in the pursuit of hard numbers. A college administrator is likely to regard his doggedness as bullying. Every year between 5 and 10 percent of schools refuse to submit data about acceptance rates, test scores, and so on. They usually make their refusals with a flourish of self-congratulation for having refused to submit to the tyranny of *U.S. News*. But the joke's always on them. Bob ranks them anyway. He finds the numbers elsewhere, or he extrapolates the school's data from other sources, and computes the ranking from those.

"We're going to publish every year, no matter what," he said. "Whether they like it or not. They know that if they don't turn in their statistical data, they're still going to be ranked. We don't back down when the schools get mad at us. So usually they figure, it might as well be our own data as someone else's data."

Bob leaves his office quite a bit, to travel the endless circuit of higher-education conferences and conventions, scouting his critics and defending the rankings and his methodology. I've seen him in public gatherings where panelists—usually high school counselors or admissions deans—spy him in the audience and go on to speak of his work in terms that wobble between contempt and outrage. Once I saw the admissions dean from Yale look down from the dais straight at Bob. "Some will say *U.S. News* is the axis of evil," the dean said, who added that he didn't quite agree with such a harsh assessment, not quite. Then he mentioned the commercialism, competitiveness, and superficiality that debased higher education in America. "You are the greatest amplifier of all these things. You force people into this," he said. "They can fight back, but you always win."

And Bob's expression never changes. He looks as woebegone as ever. He's remarkably unflappable.

"Sometimes it gets personal. 'You did this!' 'You did that!'" he said. "I don't like that. But I think I understand it. They're very frustrated—they can't figure it out. Admissions is their world, and they think it's a world they can control. And here's *U.S. News* and they think, 'How did these outsiders get so powerful over what I do for a living?' That's what they think, anyway—they think we're so powerful.

"They pretend to argue with all the statistics, but what they really hate is that we treat education as a product," he said. "And then we rank it in descending order. They hate that. But we don't do this for them—it's not for the college presidents or the academics. It's a consumer guide, for consumers."

I recalled a conversation I'd had with one of *U.S. News*'s most persistent critics, a former high school counselor named Lloyd Thacker, who helped orchestrate the peer-review boycott. After one panel where Bob and the rankings were slagged mercilessly, Thacker took me aside and said, in an anguished voice, "Education is not a commodity. Students are not customers!" It's a common theme. Most institutions of higher learning are not-for-profit, of course, and the field attracts people who for one reason or another are averse to the world of commerce, and sometimes alienated from it. When educators really want to disparage *U.S. News,* they use the term "commercial rankings"—to distinguish them, I suppose, from noncommercial rankings, of which there are none. Many have succumbed to a caricature of what commerce and businessmen are like. The university people recoil at the thought that they are producers of a consumer good (a very expensive one) rather than, as Thacker says, "guides on a journey." They cringe at the notion that their students are mere consumers rather than spiritual entities whose souls require their special nourishment. They're appalled by the unstoppable imperialism of the market—the relentless intrusion of cost-benefit logic, even into a realm that its practitioners hoped might be kept free from the market's vulgarities.

It's only natural, then, that they respond to this business mentality in the way they think businessmen would. They cheat.

BOB IS TOUGHER THAN HE looks, but he does show one symptom of shell shock from the constant barrage. He's insisted to me several times that the rankings aren't terribly influential, either with college-bound kids or with the schools themselves. "It's soooo exaggerated," he said. I think he's been accused of ruining American higher education so often that he wants to persuade you such a thing is beyond his powers. "There are studies that show this," he added, striking an assertive tone that's unusual for him—unusual for anybody, really, considering that he's boasting that social science has proved nobody takes his life's work seriously.

He's not completely right about the studies, however. The evidence is mixed. In surveys most freshmen say in hindsight that college rankings, including those of *U.S. News,* didn't have much effect on their choice of school. Among students with the highest grades and test scores, however, studies show that rankings are deemed "very important." This is especially true of their parents, two-thirds of whom called *U.S. News* rankings "very helpful." As one research summary, by Luke Myers and Jonathan Robe, put it, "While the majority of students may not consider a school's placement in a popular ranking, those with the greatest academic ability are directly or indirectly (through their parents) influenced by rankings." And those are precisely the kids colleges are trying to attract.

For schools the consequences of failure can be grim. Another study, written by James Monks and Ronald Ehrenberg and published by the National Bureau of Economic Research, showed what happens if a school slips in the rankings. It attracts fewer applicants and is forced to accept a higher percentage of them. And then it sees more of its offers declined by those who do get in. The acceptance rate goes up, the yield goes down—and the money rolls out. The study found that a declining rank leads a school to offer more "tuition discounts"—more financial aid—to bring in the customers. That means less money for library books, chem labs, teacher salaries, even hot tubs. The drop in expenditures and the rise in acceptance rate show up in the *U.S. News* data, and the school's rank slips further.

What, then, are school administrators to do? Did someone say *cheat*? Maybe a better word is *fudge*. The politest term is *gaming the system*. The first concrete evidence that administrators were gaming the *U.S. News* rankings came in 1995, in an article in the *Wall Street Journal* by a reporter named Steve Stecklow. The story would have read like a horror tale to anyone still seduced by the vision of American higher education unsullied by commerce. Stecklow showed a Hobbesian jungle of careerist bureaucrats, red in tooth and stapler claw. His method was simple and elegant. He got the bright idea of comparing the data that schools submitted to *U.S. News* with the data that they submitted to bond-rating agencies. As he pointed out, if they lied to a rating agency, they might go to jail; if they lied to *U.S. News,* they might make the Top Twenty. Reviewing credit reports for more than one hundred schools, he caught one in four fudging the numbers.

A few of the discrepancies were clerical errors; most weren't. The favorite fudgeable figure was the average SAT scores of incoming freshmen. It's an important indicator in Bob's calculations. Some schools computed their average SAT score by simply ignoring the scores of entire groups of students—the foreign-born or economically disadvantaged. Boston University included the math SAT scores of its incoming foreign-born freshmen, but not their verbal scores. Northeastern University neglected to include the scores of 20 percent of its incoming class, which had the effect, Stecklow reckoned, of boosting the school's SAT average by fifty points. Other schools had omitted the scores of athletes, minorities, and the kids of alumni ("legacies," in admissions talk). Stecklow found discrepancies in all regions of the country and in every kind of school. Harvard was implicated, and so was Bard—even the Christian Brothers at Christian Brothers University, for chrissakes.

Graduation rates were also manipulated. Schools are required to furnish graduation rates to the NCAA, and *U.S. News* asks for them too. Fifty of the 300 schools gave higher graduation rates to the magazine than to the NCAA. One almost poignant story came from a former official at Colby College, who once misreported a key class-rank indicator to *U.S. News.* The mistake was inadvertent, but it bumped Colby's rank from twentieth to fifteenth. The improbable rise in the ranking sent Colby administrators scrambling "to preserve our competitive advantage." They were forced, over the next several years, to commit "numbers massage," in the Colby administrator's delightful phrase.

The gaming continues, sometimes publicly. The most brazen campaign was undertaken by Clemson University, in South Carolina, which named James F. Barker its president in 1999. Barker pledged to climb the page: he would put his alma mater into *U.S. News* top twenty of public research universities within ten years, a big lunge from the number thirty-eight position it then occupied. By 2008, Clemson had risen to twenty-two, and the sky's the limit. Barker's success was the talk of the higher-education world.

Most presidents and deans could guess how he pulled it off. The definitive answer came in a presentation given in 2009 by the head of Clemson's research department, an insouciant woman named Catherine Watt. She described a school mobilized for an all-out assault on every indicator that Bob Morse used to rank a university. "No indicator, no method, no process [is] off limits to create improvement," Watt said in her presentation. The class-size indicator, for example: the rankings reward a school for offering classes with fewer than twenty students and penalize it for offering classes with more than fifty. Clemson's method was to find classes with enrollments right at those margins. So, say, from a class with twenty-two students, three might be moved into a class that was already over fifty. Voilà: a gain of one under-twenty class, with no increase in the number of over-fifty classes. And why not? As Watt said, a class with more than fifty students "may as well grow larger" and no harm done. The school wouldn't be penalized any worse for a class that had fifty kids or seventy or ninety. She called this "manipulation around the edges."

Another popular trick involves alumni giving. The rankings treat a school kindly if it has a high percentage of donating alums. Clemson alumni were bombarded with solicitations for even the smallest gifts, even five dollars—any amount so long as the school could report a higher percentage of active donors. The indicator for faculty salaries rose too, when the school began folding professors' benefits packages into the average salary number reported to *U.S. News.* Best of all, when the reputational survey arrived every spring, asking President Barker to rate other universities, he made sure to rank Clemson higher than every other school: Harvard, Stanford, Princeton, Yale. "I'm a hard grader," he said, when his survey results came to light.

None of these tricks was unique to Clemson, and some of them, such as a lower faculty–student ratio, probably benefited students. Bob knows he could try to nullify the effect of other fudges. But he'd only generate more criticism—another of the damned-if-you-do-damned-if-you-don't aspects of his job. He has considered changing the alumni-giving indicator, for example. Instead of simply listing what percentage of alumni donate money, he could compute the size of the average donation. "But then they'd say we were just rewarding wealthy schools," he said. "We already get enough of that."

Bob works hard to keep the schools honest. He and his data collectors cross-check the numbers where they can, and their software program rings bells when the data show an unusual jump from one year to the next. A school hoping to climb the page should make its advance at a slow and steady pace. It took Washington University more than ten years to alter its reputation as a modest Midwestern liberal arts college in St. Louis to one of the highest ranked schools in the country. Its climb relied heavily on *U.S. News* indicators, and it's still the stuff of legend among admissions professionals. In a mix of envy and awe, they are always happy to explain how it was done.

Washington University wasn't a notable school, but it was a rich one, and the rankings showed how all that money could be put to use. It recognized early on that, as Kat Cohen had said, there were a lot of valedictorians out there, and they couldn't all go to Brown. Washington resolved to soak up as many of these "high-value applicants" as possible. It directed its marketing to the footloose high achievers, but not only to them. Soliciting students nationwide, in regions and demographic categories it had never considered before, the school vastly expanded its pool of applicants. More applications meant a lower acceptance rate. To increase its yield, the school greatly increased its offers of financial aid, even for well-to-do students, and began accepting high percentages of early-decision applicants.

As the school climbed the page, the higher ranking attracted applicants with higher scores. The higher SAT average drew students with higher class rankings. The school raised money aggressively from its alumni, increasing its endowment and budget. It hired more PhDs to teach more classes, shrinking its average class size and raising the salaries of its faculty. In every rankings category it huffed and puffed until it created an updraft that was self-reinforcing. No one any longer—not even Bob, really—denies that the rankings shape the way schools use their resources, whether through manipulating their numbers or in a genuine effort to become a better school, as *U.S. News* defines a better school: smaller classes, bigger salaries, happier alumni, smarter kids.

As I was beginning to see, though, for applicants and their parents the success of *U.S. News* makes for a more complicated story. Bob told me that a great benefit of the rankings is that they let all of us be our own admissions counselors—a necessity for those who can't write the $40,000 check to Kat Cohen, especially now that the average high school counselor is hopelessly overstretched and not much help.

"People have to become self-educated about admissions," he said. "In a sense, they're on their own." Bob has labored hard to make this process as transparent as possible, and the gusher of information the magazine releases each year is impressive. And he has lots of company these days. The College Board—the organization that administers the SAT—publishes further refinements of the numbers, in print and on the Web, and the Department of Education has developed its College Navigator Web site, making even more data, piles and piles of data, about even more schools, available for free.

This is where the confusion comes in. *U.S. News*'s cracking of the dam that restricted access to large amounts of information was a revolution in college admissions. Here as elsewhere in the information age, the general release of so much material empowered ordinary people, just as all those Internet gurus said it would. Like the silicon chip and the Internet and cellular technology, it shifted power from producers to consumers, from the corporate to the individual; it flattened hierarchies and dissolved artificial boundaries, ending the tyranny of experts and middlemen and allowing us to be our own experts, to customize information to our own tastes and needs. And now that I was fully empowered, I didn't know where to begin.

I held tangible evidence of the problem when I left Bob's office and he handed me a stack of the *U.S. News* guides. It was a foot thick and weighed several pounds; the college guide alone runs to 1,800 pages. He told me my son and I might want to start sifting through the magazine's college Web site too. It had more than a hundred thousand pages of information.

"A hundred thousand pages!" I said. "Great!"

3

Do It Yourself Admissions

The price of Pee Wee soccer—
the principle of constant contradiction—
a moratorium ends—perverse effects—The Books—
alternative universes—College Confidential—
when TMI becomes TMA—the high-tech lyceum—
the trials of puppywuppy

BOB WAS right about one thing especially, as I knew from our visit to my son's preoccupied college counselor: the kid was going to have to educate himself—which meant, perforce, that my wife and I were going to have to educate ourselves, and then we'd self-educate him. That's how things work.

When I got home I dropped the slab of books on the dining-room table, placing them at an angle to a pile of even thicker books that I'd already acquired. I looked around for my son, but failing to find him, I started in on the *U.S. News* special college issue. The cover photo showed a scrum of wholesome young people, leaping about in robes and mortarboards, scarcely capable of controlling their joy. Inside there were ads for test-prep tutors and life insurance companies; several lesser-known schools had bought full-page spreads that practically screamed desperation, imploring kids to give them a look with meaningless slogans fresh from a focus group—"Discover Your True North at Ohio Northern University," "Bryant University: The Character of Success." (Somewhere, another school's focus group had suggested "The Success of Character.") And of course there were the *U.S. News* rankings themselves. I hadn't realized there were so many categories, in the special issue, in the guide, on the Web.

The *U.S. News* editors early on faced the objection that the higher-education system, with its 1,400 four-year colleges and universities, is simply too large and various to assess in a handful of ranking categories. It's unfair, for example, to put up a perfectly adequate if unselective school like Southern Illinois University, whose budget rises and falls at the whim of politicians and whose freshman class is meant to mirror the state's population by region and income, against Harvard, whose endowment tops $25 billion and whose method of admissions is to line up every smart kid in the country and then throw bags of money at the ones it wants. To do justice to the diversity of schools, the ranking categories have multiplied like a cat with kittens. The constantly expanding litter guarantees that almost any respectable school will make a semidecent showing in at least one category or other—and then be able to brag about it to alumni and parents.

I thumbed through the rankings. The possibilities for triumph seem endless. There's the Best 111 Liberal Arts Colleges, the Top Five Public Liberal Arts Colleges, the Top 100 National Universities, the Top Fifty Public National Universities, the Top Ten Master's Universities in the South, the Top Ten Baccalaureate Colleges in the Midwest, the Top Twenty-five Master's Universities in the West, and so on. There was a list for best "commitment to undergraduate teaching" and a list for best "A + Schools for B Students" and a list for "best values," and each of these lists was broken down into ten subrankings. Beyond this there were nine different categories of "Schools to Watch," two top twenty-five rankings from a poll of guidance counselors, and lists of the top schools ranked by acceptance rate, graduation rate, and proportion of classes with fewer than twenty students (Thomas Aquinas College comes in first in this ranking, with Judson College in Alabama at number seven). The sixth best baccalaureate college in the Northeast is Elmira College. Just so you know. It's like a Pee Wee soccer league, where every kid gets a trophy (Happiest Smile, Cleanest Socks). The lists were meant to be clarifying but had grown into an impenetrable jungle. There were lists of lists of lists.

I was surprised to read, in the magazine's introductory essay, this bubbly bit of Panglossianism: "Above all," the essayist said, "remember that college, any college, is going to set you well on the path for a successful career and life beyond the classroom."

Really? If college-bound Americans believed that this sentence was true—if they thought that one school was as good as another at performing its essential task—then the very magazine I was holding in my hands would go poof. All of Bob Morse's proprietary software would stutter, blink, and erase itself. Kat Cohen's fancy office building would crumble onto Fifty-seventh Street. This stack of college books on my dining-room table would implode in a cloud of dust. Our insatiable desire for data, information, numbers, inside knowledge—our pursuit of the Grail of admissions—would cease. And then we could all go back to doing something productive.

But of course we really didn't believe this. The stack of books alone was testament to the belief of American parents that somewhere out there, nestled in a green, cozy valley or rising up beyond a wrought-iron gate in a great city, was a college that more than any other would launch their sons or daughters on "a successful career and life," if they ever managed to pay off their student loans. And the consequence of this belief was the rushing currents of information and advice that I found myself in right now, none of which, it seemed to me, made our task easier. I had too much information already. Evidently I was going to need more.

AND THAT'S WHEN I STUMBLED onto the law of constant contradiction. It was to complicate our self-education from first to last. The law was this: for every piece of advice or information a parent or child receives while applying to college, there is an equal and opposite piece of advice or information that will contradict it.

Like most parents I was suddenly alert to news stories I'd never bothered to read before. For years I had considered large tracts of the daily newspaper a no-fly zone. I had my own private news blackout. I refused to read letters to the editor, the home-design section, op-eds about politics, unsigned editorials, lacrosse box scores, and any article about fishing, Canada, the obesity epidemic, or college admissions. I figured there would be plenty of time to read admissions stories when the moment arrived. And now it had. Admissions stories are a staple of the news business, of course. They have been so since the first baby boomer editor realized he couldn't afford the tuition of the school his kid desperately wanted to go to, and he dispatched his reporters to find out why the hell not. The genre was greatly encouraged by the stunning success of *U.S. News*. Now I noticed the stories were everywhere. I could scarcely keep up. Every morning at breakfast I lingered over articles in the Life section with headlines like "Acing Your Application" or "What Every Parent Needs to Know About College Admissions" or (too cutely) "How Not to Get into College."

And then the law of constant contradiction asserted itself. Any bit of advice that wasn't hopelessly lame—enjoy the process! think positive!—was soon contradicted by another piece of advice from a different source. One day I'd read in *Forbes* that "Perfect test scores may be out of reach, but a student can still create the perfect application." Not long after, the *Wall Street Journal* would tell me of another common problem: "Too many students are submitting 'professionalized' applications rendered all too slick by misguided attempts at perfection." Then, from a magazine supplement to the local paper: "Even the smallest typo or grammatical mistake can give an excuse for the reader to chuck an app."

Every now and then, I entertained the idea that I should just back off and let my son handle this whole thing. So I was glad when I found in another article a confirming quote: "Parental meddling is the curse of the applications process." I was glad only temporarily, till I read, in a family advice column: "Parents, you owe it to your high-schooler to get involved! There are things only you can do!" Yes, I thought, there are. For example: "Let the admissions officers know you're interested—don't be afraid to call or email." A week later I read about a new phenomenon that deans were complaining about. It was called "admissions stalking." This is what happens when "too many pointless emails and calls from overanxious students and parents" alienate an admissions officer. "Such efforts have no bearing on an applicant's fate."

I saved the tip for my file, along with all the others.

AND ALWAYS THERE WAS THE stack of books resting on our dining-room table, collecting ketchup stains. My wife and I tried and failed to press them on my son, who these days always seemed headed out the door when the subject of college came up—off to a basketball practice or, ingeniously, a "study session" with friends, reminding me as he went that it was more important for him to keep his grades up than to spend time reading about "college stuff." Pleading overwork, my wife was slow to commit to the process too. I was left to drift alone among The Books.

There were several volumes like Kat's, full of chatty, nail-biting pointers, with little variation from title to title. They gave off the predatory air of those pop business books sold in airport stalls, promising nervous middle managers they could unlock the secret of capitalist success by "Unleashing the Hidden Bionics of the Brand" and "Refueling Your Platform with the Power of Yes." They were short books, reasonably enough, and quick to read, though usually much longer than they needed to be. Much of the advice was too flimsy or obvious—several pages on why it's important to *proofread your app*—to allow for contradiction.

The thicker books were college guides. Unlike Bob's *U.S. News* guide, which restricted itself to listing page after page of unadorned facts about a school, these guides featured essays, sometimes several pages long, about individual colleges, alongside pullout boxes filled with data. They were designed for thumbing through and dipping into—perfect for reading in the bathroom, except you couldn't. Each guide was a thousand pages of newsprint or more, cheaply slapped between slick cardboard covers with glue-glob binding that would last just till your kid went off to school and not a moment longer. Whatever their other merits, the guides were impossible to hold comfortably in the hand. They slipped and slid. They flopped open when you wanted them closed and flipped closed when you wanted them open. No bathroom could contain them.

I stopped buying college guides after I had five of them, when I noticed that of the five, four seemed at first glance to be interchangeable. The best-selling of them all was the *Fiske Guide*. Its first edition was put out in 1982 by the education editor of the *New York Times*. Ted Fiske has retired from the *Times* but he still publishes his guide, along with companion volumes under his own eponymous brand. With the help of a small staff, Fiske mails questionnaires every few years to college administrators, who pick a handful of students—sometimes as few as five—to answer questions about college life and then return the forms to Fiske. His method is highly subjective and unscientific, as he admits without apology. "Social scientists will tell you it's crazy," he once told me. "But I don't talk to social scientists if I can help it."

With some variation, Fiske's method has been copied by nearly all his competitors: editors survey students or recent graduates by mail or over the Web, pluck quotes from the written answers, and then type up a review of each school in a breezy style. Again the formula is a sure moneymaker. It offers low overhead, high margins, a market that refreshes itself every year, and meanwhile you make the schools do all the boring stuff. The guides sell for a bit more than twenty dollars. For this sum the *Fiske Guide* claims to give you "an insider's look" at the top 310 schools. *The Insider's Guide to the Colleges*, edited by the staff of the *Yale Daily News*, gives you "an insider's look" at the 330 top schools. *Barron's Guide to the Most Competitive Colleges* gives you "an insider's assessment" of the eighty-six top schools. *The Princeton Review 368 Best Colleges* gives you the "inside word" on the top 368 schools (though the number of top schools changes mysteriously with each edition). *Choosing the Right College*, my fifth guide, is put together by conservative Republicans for other conservative Republicans, on the premise that "many college classes are little more than indoctrination in leftist propaganda." It sounded like an outsider's guide to me, but no: *Choosing the Right College* gives you "information previously only available to insiders." The number of their top schools is 134.

As it happened, the guides were not interchangeable. Flopping them open on the dining-room table, I searched for what these insiders had to say about the schools my son had expressed interest in. I started with our Big State University, BSU. I learned from the *Insider's Guide*—I know, they're all insider's guides—that BSU had a four-year graduation rate of 92 percent. From *Choosing the Right College,* I learned that BSU had an 83 percent four-year graduation rate. *Fiske* told me the strongest majors at BSU were English, Spanish, Portuguese, Religious studies, and German; I learned from *Barron's* that the strongest majors were English, history, and biology. As for the most *popular* majors at BSU, they were psychology, economics, and business—when I was reading *Princeton Review.* When I read *Barron's,* the most popular majors became psychology, history, and English.

At Notre Dame, the *Princeton Review*'s insiders told me that the school had an acceptance rate of 24 percent and a yield of 56 percent; the insiders at *Insider's Guide* said the acceptance rate was 27 percent and the yield was 16 percent. At *Choosing the Right College* the yield zoomed to 58 percent. The Notre Dame in *Choosing* had a faculty–student ratio of eleven to one, much more intimate than *Princeton Review*'s Notre Dame, where it was thirteen to one. Sometimes reading the guides was like traveling through alternative universes: not only did USC's four-year graduation rate greatly improve on its way from *Choosing* to the *Insider's Guide* (from 69 percent to 84 percent), the crime rate changed too. In the *Insider's Guide* USC "was surprisingly safe." In *Choosing the Right College* "the entire USC area" was "incredibly unsafe." Republicans are such wusses.

These discrepancies usually arose only on matters of objective importance, such as the most popular majors at a school, its acceptance rate, and the odds of getting knifed on your way to the library. When it came to the intangibles, a school's culture, the tone or texture of campus life, the law of constant contradiction was momentarily suspended. The guides showed an impressive uniformity: every school was nearly perfect. Everywhere the students "worked hard" but "knew how to party when they were done studying." Profs were all "accessible" even if occasionally "you have to seek them out"; they were also "terrific" and "awesome." There "was always something going on on campus"—on every campus, all the time. "Students do a great job balancing work and play." "Class sizes are manageable" but "it depends on the class you take." That does make sense. "If you're not afraid to work hard, you'll do fine."

I ventured beyond the schools my son was interested in, looking for variety. I didn't find it. Suddenly I was mad to read about a school where the profs were mouth-breathers and the parties were as fun as an autopsy, where psychopaths overran the fraternities and a half-asleep third grader could pass the chemistry class. But of course I never found it, not in these books. The guides insist they're describing the "top schools," after all, and it stands to reason that top schools will share certain marks of excellence, even if the excellence starts to run thin by the time you get to the 373rd top school. In choosing students to respond to the surveys, college administrators are unlikely to ask the pipehead passed out in the dormitory stairwell for his candid views. These surveys are filled out by the kind of young people who volunteer to fill out surveys—a principle of self-selection certain to yield a highly upbeat group of youngsters. Insiders are all alike, no matter what school they go to.

I once asked Ted Fiske about this positive tone, its mind-numbing consistency from review to review. It didn't seem particularly helpful to a parent or student hoping to choose one top school over another. After a while, I said, they look pretty much identical. He waved his hand.

"People say to me, 'Your book's too nice!' Okay, but guess what: most students like the schools they're in. That's why they're there. If someone does send in a harshly negative survey, well, I know a disgruntled student when I see one. Why would I use that? I want good information. If I let the schools pick the students for the surveys, that protects me against negative misinformation, the kind of thing you get from some disgruntled kid."

The guides are a commercial enterprise. They have buyers to please. My hunch is that students and their parents come to such books looking for reassurance, mostly, and they'll go away unhappy if they read that their dream school is less than they dreamed. And beyond any one school the guides were propagandizing for the very *idea* of college, as the upper middle class conceives it—the embrace of leafy campuses, the raucous but mostly wholesome parties alongside the rigors of learning, the all-nighters and dorm-room camaraderie and late-night food runs. If nothing else, The Books confirmed my admiration for Bob Morse and his aversion to subjectivity.

It also reinforced my skepticism about insiders. I wondered whether any "inside dope" could be useful or reliable. After a few days and several cursory glances through the guides, I stopped pushing them on my son. I noticed him thumbing through them once or twice as application deadlines drew near, but in time the guides came to rest on the floor in a corner of the dining room, where they stayed undisturbed, out of the way of foot traffic and stacked in a tilting tower, till my son went away to school and my wife couldn't stand the clutter anymore. Two of them came apart as I tipped them into the trash.

AROUND THE TIME I GAVE up on the college guides I spoke with my friend Rob. He and his wife had liberated themselves from the printed word altogether. Like us, they were self-educating while their son, like ours, went into a dead man's float. They had moved their investigations into cyberspace exclusively. As a consequence they had taken on the annoying traits that people who are cutting-edge often show toward those of us who are, to put it mildly, not. Rob expressed exaggerated dismay when I told him I hadn't heard of College Confidential. "Wow," he said. "Tons of good advice. I can't believe you haven't seen it."

And then, once I became aware of it, every parent I met seemed to be addicted to, or infuriated by, College Confidential. News articles have christened it the largest and most popular information resource for college admissions on the Web, or anywhere, for that matter. And it is indeed unimaginably vast. Its message board contains hundreds of thousands of posts, broken down by subject and school, with a powerful search engine that makes it easy to navigate. College professors, high school teachers, college students, alumni, even an occasional admissions counselor all chime in. But mostly the site is given over to throbbing parents and their anxious children, seeking comfort, solidarity, and advice, always more advice.

College Confidential is what happens when our terrible case of college jitters meets our Internet fixation. It's a dangerous combination, like drinking on an empty stomach. Accustomed to turning to the Web to find any elusive piece of information, whether it's the definition of "proscenium" or the value of pi to the seventh decimal, we now turn to it even for things that don't technically count as information—advice, for example. More often than not we ignore the distinction when we head to the Web. My problem with College Confidential wasn't just TMI but TMA, too much advice.

As in other areas of life, such as pornography and day trading, the Internet hasn't caused the problem, it has just made it worse. I'd been bewildered by TMA before, for reasons having nothing to do with getting my kid into college. Before a business trip I'd go online to find a recommendation for a rodent-free hotel or a reliable restaurant. Half a dozen Web sites would be waiting to help. Each would offer me pages of advice posted by anonymous advice givers. From them I learned that the local big-chain hotel was in fact a good bargain, with pleasant service and an excellent location, and also a hellhole staffed by human ferrets, with overflowing toilets and untraceable smells that had ruined the honeymoon of vox-12popula and iwantmyrum, who were now exacting their revenge by abusing the hotel on every Web site they could find.

"The worst experience of my life!" GoatHerd would say. "Boutique-y, quiet, a real charmer," said lovesavage21. Another would split the difference: "Not terrible, but you could do better for the price," said HiroshimaMonAmour. I of course had no way of knowing which advice to take. I'd search the comments for telltale clues that might indicate who was the bigger crank, GoatHerd or lovesavage21. The clues weren't there. And I'd be no better off than if I hadn't asked the question to begin with—worse, maybe.

Internet utopians like to call message boards like College Confidential a "community," which gives it a cozy feel, or a "high-tech lyceum," which gives it a pretentious one. What it is, is a Web site where people from all walks of life, from every income level and background, create a communal space without fear of reprisal and in a spirit of perfect openness, so they can spread misinformation, gossip, and lunatic conjecture to people who are as desperate as themselves. Cultural hierarchies are indeed upended, just as the utopians said they would be—for example, the tyrannical, suffocating top-down arrangement that privileges people who know what they're talking about above people who don't.

Members of the College Confidential community, it goes without saying, follow the Internet convention of using nicknames rather than given names. I may be the last person in America who hasn't gotten used to this practice. I know that thousands of intelligent people with unimpeachable expertise are publishing nuggets of wisdom on the Internet round the clock, but why do they call themselves "rodthebod" or "puppywuppy"? How seriously are we supposed to take the opinions of a person who identifies himself as "boogerman"? At College Confidential the names tend to be self-aggrandizing: "proudmama," "Harvard2400" (2400 being, of course, a perfect SAT score), "superstar," "epiphany." Like the Internet itself, the anonymity releases them not only from the stultifying habits of polite discourse but also from the obligation to express sequential thoughts. On College Confidential it's impossible to keep them to the subject at hand. Their obsessions obtrude, one obsession above all others.

A question about the International Baccalaureate program, an increasingly popular course of study in American high schools, will inspire comments after which another member complains about affirmative action. A scared kid will ask how a particular admissions committee weighs extracurricular activities, and after he receives a response or two, a member will complain about affirmative action. Another parent will float an idea about sending applications in early, provoke a few observations from other parents, and then a member will complain about affirmative action. Conversational forums on College Confidential are like water circling a drain—no matter which direction it comes from it always heads toward the same place.

In a sense, though, even affirmative action is a subset of the problem that truly consumes the questioners and advice givers on College Confidential: will someone please tell us how we can get into the college we want to get into? And the longer you linger the plainer the answer becomes: nobody can tell you because nobody knows, and nobody will admit that nobody knows. Some message threads run to well over five hundred posts, making it impossible to sift through it all—partly because it's too time-consuming, partly because it's too boring. Even so, a member may say something plausible and helpful once in a while. And then the law of constant contradiction asserts its iron will.

FOR INSTANCE: ONE EVENING WE discuss how to approach teachers for college recommendations. I repeat the advice I heard from Kat.

"It's a little late for sucking up," he says.

"It's never too late to suck up," I say. The question, I tell him, is not *when* to suck up but *how*. Do you try several teachers at once? Fill out the form yourself? Offer a crib sheet listing your accomplishments, interests, and general wonderfulness that they can use as a guide? He doesn't know and I don't either, and The Books are no help.

Still new to College Confidential, I sign on to the site and within seconds find a "recommendations" thread. And then another and another.

Every personality type is here. College Confidential is the human drama played out in pixels. You run into cocksure jocks and nervous nellies, brainiacs and dullards, know-it-alls and—well, everybody's a know-it-all on College Confidential. Once again the anonymity doesn't help. It encourages bravado. Fast27 is one of the first to answer the query about recommendations. His answer carries an impressive air of methodological expertise, like a papal bull. Fast27 is clearly a fellow who has been around the campus a few times. "Always offer [your teacher] a folder with a list of colleges, deadlines, application type, checklist, resume, cover letter, all the forms (fill out as much as you can yourself), all the envelopes—stamped and pre-addressed." And one other thing: be sure to include a gift by way of a thank-you.

Northstarmom arrives to scoff. "You don't need to get them thank you gifts." She advises against even offering a résumé to help the teacher in writing the "rec." 996GT2 agrees: "A resume is overly pretentious." A few clicks later student615 gravely announces that you should definitely give a résumé to the teacher. Cs08carolina offers personal testimony: she gave her teacher her résumé and got a much better recommendation than she would have otherwise. No, says kruschevtm, the résumé should be integrated into other materials you give the teacher, not included as a stand-alone document . . .

Suddenly the previously unknown Imathriver pops in, immodestly and unhelpfully. "Both mine were great letters of recommendation," he announces to us all. Someone called a2npersu2n takes this unprovoked boast as an insult. "Dude," he says, "I can assure you my recommendations were amazing."

Plattsburghloser tries to get the conversation back on track. She says she sure did give her teacher a gift and she can't imagine what would have happened if she hadn't. The rec was superb! Pearlygate expresses disgust at this, saying the gift was nothing more than a thinly disguised bribe. Wounded, plattsburghloser responds: "It wasn't as if I'd bought him a new Porsche." This is the last we hear from her, for she has crept silently away. Then a2npersu2n and Imathriver reappear. They're still bickering about whose recommendations were more awesome. They pelt each other with angry emoticons. Then arabrab says you'd have to be crazy not to give your recommending teacher a résumé. But by then most of us have lost the thread.

And an hour has passed—an hour that has gone from my life forever, an hour I will never get back. I tell my son what I've learned, or rather what I haven't learned. He seems unsurprised.

When he finally asks a teacher for a recommendation, my son asks him whether he wants a résumé to look over before he writes, or a crib sheet, or a draft letter, or what. The teacher tells him what he needs. After so much time with College Confidential this simple method strikes me as quaint—as distant in time as a rotary dial phone. Just ask! Get an answer!

Advice is only useful if you can't ask everyone for advice about everything.

4

PUT TO THE TEST

Agony in the chair-desk—
catching up with an old bully—bricks for brains—
luxury in Princeton—the origins of the test—
Conant's dream—a sorting mechanism—
firing the doctor—the privilege of privilege—
the end of aptitude

IT WAS a bright, breezy morning of drifting sunlight and cho-
rusing birds, so I decided to ruin it by taking the SAT. College
Confidential offered lots of advice about the SAT, of course, the
inside word on when to take it and how to prepare for it and how
to outsmart the nerds who write the questions. Before the April
test date, my son considered enrolling for classes with the venerable
Stanley H. Kaplan test preparation service (now known, like Cher
and Shrek, by the simple monomial: Kaplan), so I went looking for
a thread, without knowing why, and, without surprise, found it.

Voodoo santa advised, "sat prep courses aren't as good as self
studying." Godfatherbob agreed.

Legend.dracula said, "kaplan is bad." He told us to spend our
money on PR, Princeton Review test prep, instead.

"Kaplan is excellent," said Baelor. "Pr is actually worse."

"Don't take Kaplan," said karianasgun. "Don't take PR."

Having cleared that up, my son decided to register with Kaplan because a friend was taking the class.

I WAS MOVED TO TAKE the test myself in part by parental fellow feeling. An hour and a half after dawn I had dropped the boy off into a swarm of teenagers hiving at the entrance of the local high school. There they waited for the great glass doors to swing open so they could slip into the seat of a flimsy pink-and-blue polypropylene combo chair-desk. Then they would open their test booklets, grip their sharpened number two pencils, and submit themselves to the SAT. They would carefully mark only one answer for each question, and they would make sure to fill the entire circle darkly and completely. They would not make any stray marks on their answer sheet. If they erased, they would do so completely, because incomplete erasures may be scored as intended answers. If they finished before time is called, they would check their work on that section. They would NOT turn to any other section.

And this is how they would determine the course of the rest of their lives.

At least that's what a lot of them believed they were doing— my son among them, I think—and my heart went out to them, and to him. Waiting at the doors, they all looked slightly lost, as if the combination of early-morning sleepiness and the significance of what they were about to do had settled around them like a fog. I learned later the real reason they were disoriented was that they had been told they couldn't bring their cell phones into the building—none of them had gone four hours without sending a text message since middle school.

When I got home I made a cup of coffee and sharpened a packet of pencils—number twos, of course. I pulled a thick workbook from the shelf and settled myself in the sunlight at a table on our back porch. I'd gotten the workbook from my son, who had gotten it from Kaplan, which furnished all its students with fat compilations of real SATs to use for practice. The book, like the company, was an artifact of the gluttonous industry that surrounds the SAT, fed by the same anxieties that stirred my son and that still had the power to stir me—as the clutch of my stomach testified when I glimpsed the command stripped across the bottom of the cover: "DO NOT OPEN THIS BOOK UNTIL THE SUPERVISOR TELLS YOU TO DO SO."

Most of my friends can remember their SAT scores, even the really old ones (friends, not scores). I can't and don't need to. My recollection of the day when I took the test is vivid enough. I recall the classroom on a bright Saturday morning in spring, the odd feeling of being in school on a Saturday; I recall the combo chair-desk next to an open window and the sweet breeze lifting the clippings from a lawn mower that buzzed just beneath, triggering allergic reactions of epic fury; recall the swelling eyes, the twitching membrane, the postnasal tickle that made it impossible to concentrate and forced me to watch, with rising panic and snuffling groans, as my life and hopes for college drifted away. So I thought at the time, anyway. I know I bombed the SAT—but I decline to remember anything more specific than that.

The pages of the book before me now looked unpleasantly familiar—as though I had bumped into a grade school bully I hadn't seen in thirty years. The answer sheet, printed on pulpy newsprint, was just the same: still stamped with the rows of little ovals, massed in military formation, waiting for me to fill in the wrong one. But there'd been changes too, the most dramatic one appearing right up front, on the second page. In the old days the test alternated sections on math with sections covering reading ability, vocabulary, and grammar; from numbers to words and back again. This SAT opened with an essay question. The test takers are given two lined pages to fill with crisp, beguiling prose, and twenty-five minutes to do it in.

The instructions had that brisk tone I'd long remembered—the tone of a not-very-nice adult trying to act friendly with the young-sters, with only intermittent success until exasperation forces him to, goddammit, raise his voice. "Your essay must be written on the lines provided on your answer sheet—you will receive no other paper on which to write." Understood? "Try to write or print so that what you are writing is legible." Please: don't be your usual slob self. "You will have enough space if you write on every line, avoid wide margins, and keep your handwriting to a reasonable size." Reasonable. That means not too big. Okay?

Then suddenly, the SAT voice intensified with bold letters under "IMPORTANT REMINDERS: An off-topic essay will receive a score of zero . . ." Zero? "An essay written in ink will receive a score of zero." Another zero? "DO NOT WRITE ON ANOTHER TOPIC. AN OFF-TOPIC ESSAY WILL RECEIVE A SCORE OF ZERO."

And now enjoy your test and have a nice day.

I set our kitchen timer to twenty-five minutes and turned the page and looked at the essay question. "Think carefully about the issue presented in the following quotation," it said. The quote came from a writer named Patricia Moyes. "Consider the trifling causes that lead to great events," she wrote; think, for example, how an offhand remark might lead to "some resounding climax."

"Assignment: Do small events lead to catastrophes or are great events initiated by other causes? Plan and write an essay in which you develop your point of view on this issue."

After years of listening to political rhetoric, I've developed a stubborn disdain for either/or questions like this. The correct answer is usually: both. Or, just as often, neither. ("My friends, will America stick her head in the sand or stride forth to meet our chal-lenges confidently and wisely?") Yes, I thought, small events do lead to catastrophes, sometimes. And sometimes small events just stay small and then peter out. That's when great events get initiated by bigger causes, since all the small ones have gone pffft. So what of it? What kind of issue is this anyway?

72

The timer ticked. I had laid four or five sharpened number two pencils on the table in front of me, barrel to barrel like a river raft. I picked one up and angled the tip into the soft newsprint. "The relationship between cause and effect," I wrote, "can seem arbitrary, depending on our point of view . . ." and to the *chit-chit, chit-chit* beat of the timer I was off. Lucky for me, I'd recently been pawing my way through a history of the First World War before dozing off at night, and if ever there was a catastrophe (worldwide bloodbath) with a trifling cause (shooting of inbred Austrian archduke), it was WWI. I found myself unexpectedly inspired, inspired to the point of writer's cramp. It'd been a long time since I wrote by hand continuously for twenty-five minutes. When I concluded the essay, it was with a question of my own, one that I thought nicely captured the ambiguity of the topic and served as a piquant summary of my *pensée.* "Great oaks come from the smallest acorns," I wrote. "But where do the acorns come from?"

I popped up from the table, pleased, and decided to reward myself with a fresh cup of coffee. Ten minutes later the Mr. Coffee was hissing and gurgling and dripping a fresh pot of brew and I was scanning the box scores from spring training, when I remembered that I had three more hours of test to take. This is another way that an adult's life is different from a high school student's: no proctors to tell you to stop screwing around.

I hustled back to my seat at the table. There were nine more sections to go, ranging in length from ten to twenty-five minutes. I set the timer again. Next was a math section, not my favorite. I had some faith in my ability to handle long division and long multiplication, a faith that was reinforced when I saw the note at the top of the page: the use of a calculator is permitted. This was certainly an improvement from my day, when calculators were the size of a defibrillator paddle and just as expensive. I got a calculator from my son's bedroom, but when I turned to the problems themselves, I saw that none, so far as I could discern, involved long division or long multiplication. I flipped through the rest of the test. Page after page was strewn with x's and y's in weird combinations, bunched into equations and wrapped in parentheses, crouched under slash marks, sneaking around the corners of triangles, all of them laid out in a line and marching straight into a question mark, as if to say, "*Well?*"

For all I knew they could have been cuneiform. I had no idea I had forgotten so much, and wondered, while I was at it, how much I'd ever known to begin with. "Remember: All numbers are real numbers," the instructions advised. I thought hard. I knew "real number" was a math term of art—a nerd term of art. Aren't all numbers real? What could an unreal number be? I'd never been confident handling numbers, real or unreal—a fact attested to by a trail of unbalanced checkbooks stretching back thirty years—but my facility had degenerated even further since my senior year in high school, when I last had turned my attention to quantifiable problems. From then to now I'd been a word person exclusively, managing to make a living without ever having to trouble myself with integers, factors, quotients, prime numbers, or any of the other mysteries that were staring at me from the page. As a consequence, entire quadrants of my brain had turned to brick. I felt it physically, a large, dense inert mass at the center of my cranial cavity.

"The square of the result of adding 7x and y is equal to the result of subtracting the square root of 4x from y. Which of the following is an equation for the statement above?"

I looked at the multiple-choice possibilities and thought hard again, and then harder still. Nothing. It was like trying to melt concrete. I strained and nothing moved. My wordy imagination was overrun with constipation metaphors. The booklets I'd read all insisted that you shouldn't waste time on questions you could only guess at; wrong answers are deducted from your score. You should move right along to the ones where you've got a fighting chance, and return to the others as time permits. It's a sound method. But it left me with lots of free time. I went through the twenty questions in less than ten minutes because I left fourteen of them blank. At the end of the section I saw the familiar injunction. "IF YOU FINISH BEFORE TIME IS CALLED, YOU MAY CHECK YOUR WORK ON THIS SECTION ONLY. DO NOT TURN TO ANY OTHER SECTION IN THE TEST." I had fifteen minutes to go, so I doubled back, hoping to shoot the wounded. "If x and y are positive numbers and $7x/y = 3$, then which of the following equations is NOT true?" Skip it. "The square of the result of adding 7x and y is equal to . . ."

At length the timer chimed and I raised my head from my hands, where it had been resting quietly. I rose to wash the breakfast dishes, defiantly aware that I was again violating the time restrictions. When I returned to the table I consoled myself knowing that the next two sections were what used to be called the "verbal" part of the test, now known as "critical reading." A lot of the questions were straightforward vocabulary. Others involved absorbing some piece of writing and answering questions about it. I didn't think these were too difficult but they were dull—even my general anxiety about doing well on the test couldn't keep me engaged reading the long, very long passages of homogenized prose. Only one (a brief biographical sketch of Patrick Henry) conveyed any hard information that might catch on the quivering tendrils of a test taker's brain. The rest were milksop opinion: two competing passages, for example, debated whether we the people are too credulous in accepting scientific findings. The verdict? A resounding *Yeah maybe.* Sometimes we are. Sometimes we aren't, though.

In fact, all the verbal portions of the test were equally limp. After a while, nervousness was less a threat to my performance than narcolepsy.

I HAD TO KEEP REMINDING myself, as I plowed my way through one section after another, that this boring test, this heaping mass of tedium, is, paradoxically, the most passionately controversial element in the world of college admissions. That something so dull could have an effect so pyrotechnical is hard to credit. It's as if the Trojan War had been fought over Bette Midler.

The seemingly innocuous essay question is a good example. It was made a permanent part of the SAT in 2005, which means that now a perfect score is 2400, rather than the more familiar 1600. The decision to include the essay immediately became a matter of ferocious argument and second-guessing. How could something as subjective as an essay be standardized? Wouldn't the supposed scientific objectivity of the test be endangered? Could it be graded with any precision, especially on the thick-fingered scale of one (meaning totally off topic or barely literate) to six (meaning clear and persuasive)? And how could writing ability be fairly judged on the basis of a first draft, hastily jotted down in less than half an hour, under the pressure of test day and the grogginess of early morning? And what about creativity—would a freethinking student be penalized for employing unconventional forms of expression? Several years into the era of the SAT essay question, a significant number of college admissions deans—as many as 70 percent, by some estimates—still decline to consider an applicant's writing score in their decisions.

Nearly everything about the SAT, I learned, is a matter of ferocious argument and second-guessing, and has been for forty years; the essay question was merely the latest provocation in an ongoing war between the enemies of standardized testing and those who, with varying degrees of enthusiasm and conviction, defend the SAT as an essential instrument in college admissions. The claims made for and against are extravagant. You'll hear that the SAT can wreck a person's future, even if only temporarily, or salvage a bright future from a misspent past. The SAT can enforce class hierarchies or break them open; it unfairly allocates society's spoils and sorts the population into haves and have-nots, or it can unearth intellectual gifts that our nation's atrocious high schools have managed to keep buried. It is a tool of understanding, a cynical hoax, a triumph of social science, a jackboot on the neck of the disadvantaged.

Rarely, though, is it just a test. Even the College Board, which administers the SAT, and the Educational Testing Service (ETS), which designs it each year, are sheepish about using the word. SAT was originally an acronym for Scholastic Aptitude Test. When critics objected to the word "aptitude," for reasons we'll consider in a moment, SAT came to stand for Scholastic Assessment Test. Marketers soon enough realized that "test" and "assessment" have pretty much the same meaning, making "SAT" a kind of solecism, one of those repetitive redundancies that repeats itself redundantly—bad form for a test that's supposed to measure verbal ability. So they gave up trying to make an acronym altogether. "Assessment" was dropped, and so was "test," and "scholastic" too. Today the SAT is officially just the SAT; the letters don't stand for anything, as if the test makers were too timid to declare what they're up to.

And you can't blame them. The SAT is a flash point where questions of class and culture, wealth and politics, race and gender, the purpose of higher education and even our varying definitions of merit rub against one another and throw sparks when they don't burst into flames. And then there's always someone happy to fan the flames when they appear—professional activists who are devoted to destroying the SAT.

A WEEK OR SO BEFORE I managed to screw up the test for the second time in my life, I gave one of these activists a call. I was aware of the critique of the SAT only in the barest outline, but I rather liked thinking that the reason I flunked was not my own stupidity but the stupidity of the test. Bob Schaeffer is the public education director of the National Center for Fair and Open Testing. Known as FairTest, with that typographically problematic but faddish *T* capitalized in midword, the center has worked for nearly thirty years to "uncover the biases, misuses and 'coachability'" of college entrance exams. The headquarters are in a drab office in a down-market neighborhood of Boston, thanks to a shoestring budget that's just barely covered by the Ford Foundation and other stalwarts of American liberalism.

Bob's tireless work has made him the country's least avoidable critic of standardized testing, the nemesis in particular of the ETS, the College Board, and the SAT. He's a constant scold, appearing at conferences, seminars, and professional associations, plotting with other activists and peppering education reporters with an endless stream of alerts and FYIs. Like most successful political activists, Schaeffer is eternally vigilant. At the slightest cue he will unfurl his standard to its full length. When I told him on the phone that I was interested in the SAT, he spoke for more than ten minutes without a break. He dwelled particularly on the College Board and the ETS, which he sees as a cynical elite fattening on the anxieties of children and their parents by marketing a corrupt and demonstrably worthless test.

"Check out their tax returns," he said. "You'll see what we're talking about here. Executives making hundreds of thousands of dollars a year; three, four, five hundred thousand dollars. They've got, what, twenty-three vice presidents? They own their own building, the College Board does, directly across from Lincoln Center in midtown Manhattan. I've been there. Very nice. Very, very nice. Plush carpets. Art on the walls."

ETS was even worse.

"I've been to their headquarters too. They say it's in Princeton but really it's in Lawrenceville, next door. Princeton is just the mailing address, a PO box, purely for prestige. Lawrenceville doesn't sound quite as impressive, does it? But you should see it. They're located on a former equestrian farm. They have bridle paths, a goose pond, rolling hills. The director lives in the manor house—rent-free. The director they have now—not even an educator. He's a former drug salesman! His salary"—here Bob's voice slowed—"in excess of one million dollars."

When Bob and I met later for a drink, he had a chance to elaborate his critique beyond the corruptions of class and wealth. He's a numbers man by training. His hostility to the test is rooted not only in his reading of the statistical evidence but personal experience too.

"What does the SAT measure?" he asked me rhetorically. "It measures how well you do on the SAT. I say this from the perspective of being one of the world's best test takers. I could ace the written part of the Golf Pro Licenses Exam if you gave me a week to look at it. But I couldn't hit a golf ball straight."

Bob's experience with the SAT, like mine, predated the modern test-prep industry. "The drinking age back then was eighteen, and in rural Long Island, where I'm from, you could drink as long as you didn't look under sixteen. Nobody thought about test prep. Test preparation meant you sobered up the night before so you wouldn't be hungover when you took the test." His gift for scoring high on standardized tests got him to MIT, where he was surrounded by other high scorers. "I thought I was a boy genius."

Then a school project involved him with students from North Shore Community College—not high scorers.

"Some of these kids, they were smarter than the MIT kids," he said. Then he caught himself and gave me a sidelong glance: "Whatever 'smarter' means. I mean they were better at some things than the MIT kids."

Yet they'd been doomed to a crowded, poorly funded two-year community college in the shadow of MIT's ivory tower—cut off from the more prestigious university's guaranteed passage into the upper class and the American elite.

"I saw there were skill sets that these MIT kids didn't have. That convinced me: I'm not really a boy genius. I'm just a good test taker." He began studying the subject of academic testing and uncovering its sordid history.

"There is no question that the original components of standardized testing were racist, misogynist, and anti-Semitic. They believed that blue-eyed, Western European people were superior to the various other groups—my ancestors"—Schaeffer is Jewish—"and most of the people you see on the street. And they built tests that reinforced that.

"I'm not saying the people writing the test today are racist. But I don't think it matters whether they are or not. It's there in the test."

An amazingly large number of people who work in higher education agree with Bob and share his disdain. They despise both the test itself and the uses to which it is put—usually by themselves.

I WAS SEEING A PATTERN emerge in the college craziness, a kind of schizophrenia. The "corruptions" that distort college admissions are abetted by the people who are most outraged by them. The colleges that complain about the competitiveness unleashed by the *U.S. News* rankings also complain that their ranking is too low. They complain about the marketing "arms race" that reduces college to a commercial product even as they devise new marketing schemes to nab applicants from the competition. And the SAT, the most well-known and popular mechanism for judging college applicants, is publicly despised by the professionals who use it most.

I still wasn't sure whether these were instances of irony, paradox, mental illness, or hypocrisy. I did see that the work done by Bob and his allies against the SAT had found a receptive audience and was having some effect. Thanks in part to Bob's backstage consulting, the professional organization for college counselors—called NACAC, the National Association for College Admission Counseling—released a report calling on its members to take steps to decommission the test for use at their schools. When the report was presented at the group's annual convention, in 2008, the only complaints came from people who thought it didn't go far enough. "It's a lousy test," one NACAC member said heatedly on the convention floor. "It's destructive of what all of us here are trying to do."

And every year a few more schools take the step. Bob keeps a list of degree-granting institutions that have gone "test optional"— that is, they no longer require applicants to take the SAT and submit the scores, though the applicants can do so if they want. Mostly Bob's list comprises for-profit schools like DeVry University or arts academies like Juilliard, but some of the names on the list are well known—Bates, Bowdoin, Wake Forest—and when they strike their blow against the SAT they're happy to let the rest of us know they're very proud of themselves for doing so.

"By opening doors even wider to qualified students from all backgrounds and circumstances," Wake Forest's president announced in an op-ed in the *Washington Post,* "we believe we are sending a powerful message of inclusion and advocating for democracy of access to higher education."

The test, he wrote, is too "coachable": kids who can afford to will hire private tutors to boost their scores. As a result, richer students score higher on the SAT than poorer students on average. And this is just one of the "achievement gaps" that researchers have long noticed among test takers. Asian Americans—again, on average—perform better than whites on standardized tests, whites better than Hispanics, Hispanics better than African Americans, and, at least in math, men better than women. The SAT critics take any such gap as conclusive evidence of some crippling defect in the test—and a sufficient reason to eliminate it from college admissions.

Like so many widely shared beliefs in the world of higher education, this argument is seldom challenged, even though it's a relatively novel view. When the "achievement gaps" in SAT scores were first being discussed forty years ago, most liberal educators defended standardized tests. In their book *The Academic Revolution,* published in 1968, the sociologists Christopher Jencks and David Riesman famously (famously for sociologists) expressed what was then still the majority view.

"Those who look askance at testing should not rest their case on the simple notion that tests are 'unfair to the poor,'" they wrote. "Life is unfair to the poor. Tests merely measure the results."

Jencks and Riesman weren't fatalists about this state of affairs; they thought remedial programs in primary and secondary schools might help close the gap, and measures reducing income inequality would be even more successful. Still, they said, the gaps themselves weren't reason enough to abandon the tests or to dismiss a university's interest in the aptitude that the SAT measured. Do you fire your doctor because you don't like his diagnosis?

Riesman and Jencks reminded their readers how it was that standardized tests like the SAT became essential to college admissions in the first place. Notwithstanding its ancestral ties to racism and eugenics—the ties that Bob likes to remind us of—the SAT was introduced by progressive educators to accomplish the same goals that our contemporary educators now say it impedes: democratizing higher education, uplifting the poor, ending the class spoils system, and making merit rather than accidents of birth the ticket to success.

Meeting Schaeffer and talking to NACAC members, and then reading Riesman and Jencks and immersing myself in the history of the SAT, I saw why it cuts so close to our cultural vitals.

THE SAT FIRST BECAME POPULAR in the 1930s, when one side won an argument about college admissions and the other side lost. The argument was over how administrators should choose the students who would attend their schools—and who would, by extension, enter the country's leadership class in politics, business, and religion, at a time when fewer than 2 percent of American adults held degrees beyond high school. In the nineteenth century, young people hoping to attend college submitted themselves to interviews with school faculty or took essay exams that the faculty concocted. In 1900 a consortium of East Coast colleges formed the Collegiate Entrance Examination Board, the forerunner of today's College

Board, to write and disseminate "achievement tests" as a way of standardizing admissions from one school to another. The tests assessed knowledge of English grammar and literature, American and ancient history, Latin and classical Greek—the fundamentals of the prep school curriculum, the things that every educated gentleman was presumed to know. A high score virtually guaranteed a college education.

The system of achievement tests worked well for a while. But before long the blue bloods at Columbia, Harvard, and elsewhere were alarmed to discover that a disproportionate number of high scorers were not People Like Us. Many of them, indeed, were Jews. As Jerome Karabel tells the story in his magisterial history of college admissions, *The Chosen,* administrators quickly adapted. Personal interviews became a common means of screening applicants. And the criteria for admissions were mysteriously enlarged beyond high scores and good grades. Admissions officers claimed to weigh intangible qualities like "leadership," "breeding," "character," and "well-roundedness."

Here, courtesy of Karabel, is a typology of applicants that Harvard admissions officers developed privately in the 1920s. Among the types:

> Cross country style—steady man who plugs and plugs
> and plugs, won't quit when most others would . . .
> Boondocker—unsophisticated rural background . . .
> Taconic—culturally depressed background, low-
> income . . .
> Mr. School—significant extracurricular and perhaps
> (but not necessarily) athletic participation, plus
> excellent academic record.

You can guess which types Harvard preferred, no matter how well they did on the achievement tests.

Progressives of the era knew that these "objective methods"

were just a dodge—a high-minded way of keeping the riffraff out, dividing the applicant pool between Our Kind and everyone else. One of those progressives, James B. Conant, was appointed president of Harvard in 1933. A product of a shabby-genteel Yankee family himself, Conant was the chief theorist and propagandist for the "meritocratic ideology," as some historians call it, which became the declared standard for selective college admissions in midcentury America: access to an elite education should be based on academic ability rather than wealth or family background. Conant's view wasn't really an ideology so much as an ideal—one violated almost as often as it was honored, as today's progressives point out.

But still it was an ideal, and even often-ignored ideals have power to shape events. Conant despised inherited privilege and the stratagems used to sustain it. (A pet cause of his was the 100 percent inheritance tax.) He was a scientist by training, convinced that reality could be grasped objectively and quantified. And he was a true (small-*d*) democrat. He assumed that cognitive ability— the trait that made a man do well in school and, in time, might make him economically productive, a solid citizen, even perhaps a leader—could be identified and measured. He assumed that this ability, unlike economic power, was distributed equally across the population. His duty was to seek it out, and a well-wrought test would help him do it.

But not the tests that were being used in college admissions at the time, at Harvard and elsewhere. Tests of knowledge—achievement tests—by their very design worked against the meritocratic ideal, because they favored the members of one class over another. Who but the sons of privilege would do well on tests drawn from the curriculums of prep schools where only the sons of privilege were taught? Far more promising, Conant believed, was the new test of scholastic aptitude being developed by the College Board. The SAT claimed to measure not a grasp of facts but the acuteness of intelligence. It leveled the advantage that elite high schools gave their students by measuring the capacity to learn rather than learning itself. In time, Conant thought, the SAT could become a means to reward innate talent and break down the barriers to admission that wealth and privilege had put up. A favorite phrase of his was "diamonds in the rough," used to describe the jewel-like abilities lurking out there in the high schools of the vast Republic, in the intelligent kid hidden away in a bad school, or in a bright boy with bad grades.

The SAT was built for mass use. It was based on the multiple-choice tests the army had administered to draftees in World War I; those tests were likewise based on the infamous IQ tests developed, with racist intent, a generation before. The army draftees of 1917 made for a human jambalaya unlike any the country had ever seen. The draft had roped in two million farm boys, city boys, math whizzes, boulevardiers, dullards, bookworms, sharpies, poets, roués. . . . The army thought a mass testing program—the largest ever undertaken—would identify their abilities, or the lack of them, and channel the men into the military tasks to which they were best suited. Whatever their fairness and accuracy, the tests were judged useful by the officers who relied on them, and they were seized on by businessmen and educators in the era of "scientific management" that followed the war.

By the time Conant took them up, the tests had been expanded into two sections, verbal and mathematical. The twin measures gave colleges room to choose which kind of student they wanted to attract, word men or numbers men. The tests were refined year to year, and with each revision, said the College Board, the similarities to the earlier IQ tests faded. The first SATs were pitiless with time: ninety-seven minutes to answer 315 questions. The questions were no pillow fight either. One early set of problems laid out an artificial language, complete with grammatical rules and vocabulary, and required the test taker to translate English sentences into it. The time limits were eventually loosened, and "puzzle-solving" problems were replaced by reading comprehension questions—which seemed a purer test of verbal facility, and less susceptible to coach-able tricks.

Conant's embrace of the SAT gave it a kind of informal certi-fication among American educators, who even then were in thrall to Harvard College's mesmeric spell. After World War II, the test became unavoidable. The GI Bill flooded admissions offices with applicants. The College Board formed the Educational Testing Ser-vice to develop the test, while the CB continued to market and administer it. Together they greatly eased the burden on admis-sions deans. They offered the test nationwide on common dates under uniform, closely monitored conditions and furnished eas-ily understandable scores. The SAT had the reassuring look of a scientific enterprise; ETS hired superb statisticians who produced a gusher of data testifying to the exam's reliability and its yearly molting of imperfections. And the test was a bargain, at least for the schools; then as now, the College Board charged a fee from the kids who were required to take the tests and not from the colleges that required the kids to take them.

Most appealing, though, was the Conant ideal: the SAT was thought to democratize and objectify what would otherwise have been a chaotic and arbitrary process of selection, open to favoritism and corruption. It offered beleaguered admissions officers a way to assess applicants that was not only accurate but fair, untainted by class or wealth. And it had almost no competition. In 1959, test writers from the University of Iowa created the ACT (American College Testing, once upon a time, but now just an acronym like SAT), which came to be seen as a rival to SAT. The ACT more closely resembled an achievement test, tied to high school curricu-lums in Iowa, and for the next forty years it did little to dent the popularity of the SAT, particularly among private colleges, and par-ticularly in the East.

The triumph of the SAT was complete in 1968, when the Univer-sity of California, with its dozen campuses and tens of thousands of students, made it a requirement for admission for most applicants.

This solidified the test's place in popular culture. It was a symbol of the American way of success, the level playing field, the belief that prosperity was within the reach of everyone regardless of birth. And more than a symbol: self-appointed "social observers"—nice job, by the way—ascribed to the test miraculous powers and mythic importance. The journalist Nicholas Lemann, who wrote a comprehensive history of the SAT, called it "the basic mechanism for sorting the American population." And he wasn't alone in this view, he wrote: "It is almost universally taken to be today . . . a means of deciding who would reap America's rich material rewards."

This is an overblown way of describing a real trend. With high school education nearly universal, a college degree became an increasingly important marker of talent and ability, and a degree was hard to come by if you didn't take the SAT. The trend didn't make the test the "gatekeeper" Lemann and others said it was. But the exaggerations served the interests of everyone involved—except the test taker, who felt more acutely than ever the pressure of a one-shot chance at success. The College Board and ETS enjoyed the inflated view because it made them seem indispensable, even as they protested halfheartedly (as they still do) that test scores should be only one factor among many that admissions officers consider. Admissions officers were reassured by the guidance that hard numbers provided. The wildly growing test-preparation industry got rich off the student's fear of failure. And journalists and conspiracists were delighted to discover, in the CB-ETS combine, an ominous new cabal of white guys rigging the game of life to their own advantage.

Exposés of the SAT became a commonplace of populist journalism. As Riesman and Jencks had anticipated, the attacks came along lines of race and class. "For all its sermonizing about equal opportunity," wrote another journalist, David Owen, in another angry book-length exposé called *None of the Above,* "ETS is the powerful servant of the privileged." Coming from the left, the attacks seemed odd, directed as they were against a test that only a generation earlier had been installed as the quintessential liberal reform.

But they nicely illustrated a larger rupture in the country's cultural politics. The old progressivism was being abandoned by the new progressives, who saw Conant's meritocratic ideal as at best a delusion or, at worst and more likely, a swindle. Their evidence was the achievement gap. While the CB and ETS said they worked hard to ensure that everyone who took the SAT took the same test, everyone didn't get the same score. And when the scores were grouped by the race, class, or sex of the test takers—as opposed to their hair color, religion, or shoe size—they began to show the pattern mentioned earlier: Asians before whites, Hispanics before blacks, rich before poor, and men before women, except in the sections where women were before men.

You could react to this pattern in one of three ways. Option one is to ask what relevance group numbers had in a country, and an educational system, where merit is supposed to attach to individuals, not groups. Option two is to note that the data reveal that some test takers—owing to their schools, their family lives, their neighborhoods, the social services they were provided, the expectations of parents and friends—had been less prepared for college than other test takers and, as a result, had a slimmer chance of doing well in some colleges than other colleges. Option three is to insist that something is wrong with the test.

The activists chose number three. They wanted to fire the doctor.

FROM HERE THE STORY OF the SAT becomes the familiar one of an American institution, the College Board together with ETS, struggling to make itself acceptable to activists and enthusiasts who will never, under any circumstances, find the institution acceptable. It's hard to feel sorry for entities as flush and bureaucratic as the ETS and the CB. Still there's pathos in the strenuous efforts they have made in appeasing their critics, especially when you consider how slippery the critics' case can be. Instances of actual bias within the test itself have always been hard to come by. The most famous example, cited in nearly every extended critique of the SAT, was a so-called analogy question involving, of all things, the sport of rowing. The question was part of a test of verbal reasoning, and the form it took required the test taker to relate pairs of words to each other: "a runner is to a marathon as a——— is to a———." Four choices were given. The correct answer was "oarsman/regatta." The question's bias against poorer kids is pretty clear: anyone raised around the boathouse had an automatic advantage in getting the question right.

The regatta question is still held up as a sign of the obtuseness of the test designers, even though it was dropped from the test forty years ago. For that matter, all analogy questions have been eliminated, from fear of putting some test takers at a disadvantage. Since 1970, the ETS has built an intricate bureaucratic apparatus to try to cleanse each question—or "item," as a test question is called—of anything offensive or unfair.

Before a test is assembled, according to ETS guidelines, four separate reviewers examine every item for efficacy and bias. Then the item goes to a specially trained "sensitivity reviewer" who also scrubs it for any phrasing or inference that might offend a test taker. If a sensitivity reviewer objects to an item, the writer responsible for it can appeal the objection, and the case goes to another team of sensitivity reviewers for adjudication. And finally, once the test has been taken, the answers given by all test takers to each question are tabulated to see if any item "tended to cause inordinate differences [in the number of correct answers] between people in different groups . . ." If it did, "it is discarded or revised and reviewed again."

At first, in the 1970s, "different groups" was defined by socio-economic status, sex, and race, but the list has lengthened over the decades to include ethnicity and much else. Subgroups today include "older people," people with disabilities, and "people who are bisexual, gay, lesbian, or transgendered." The sensitivity guidelines are quite detailed. Word problems on math sections need to be checked for "unnecessarily difficult language" that might trip up a math whiz who's not a native English speaker. Charts and graphs are forbidden because they are difficult to reproduce in Braille. The term "hearing impaired," to describe people whose hearing is impaired, is discouraged in favor of "deaf and hard of hearing." Test writers must steer clear of the words "normal" and "abnormal." "Hispanic" should not be used as a noun, and neither should "blind"; "black" can be used only as an adjective. "Penthouse," "polo," and other "words generally associated with wealthier social classes" are likewise off-limits; "regatta," too, needless to say, along with any mention of luxuries or pricey financial instruments like junk bonds. "Elderly" is to be avoided in describing people who are elderly. "America" can't be used to describe the United States. "In general, avoid using *we* unless the people included in the term are specified. The use of an undefined *we* implies an underlying assumption of unity that is often counter to reality." Point taken.

Test writers are equally rule bound in their treatment of subject matter. Items cannot touch on military topics, sports, religion, hunting, evolution, or any other material that might be "upsetting." In fact, violence is out altogether, though some exceptions are allowed, even if they upset the vegan community. "For example, it is acceptable to discuss the food chain even though animals are depicted eating other animals."

The guidelines get ever tighter. The number of mentions of men must be balanced by the number of mentions of women. The guidelines stipulate that "20 percent of the items that mention people represent African American people, Asian American people, Latino American people, and/or Native American people." If the item doesn't allow for the test writer to identify people explicitly by race or ethnicity, he should use "place holder names" commonly associated with "various groups": Latisha or Juan or Matsuko. But sometimes a placeholder name isn't good enough, for the status of the men or women mentioned in an item must be balanced too: if you mention Albert Einstein in an item, according to the guidelines, you will not achieve gender balance simply by mentioning some anonymous "Emily" or "Imani" in the next item. You need to mention a woman of equivalent status to Einstein. Madame Curie, maybe. Sally Ride. I don't know.

Imagine tiptoeing through this minefield eight hours a day! Yet the record shows not a single instance when an ETS test writer snapped and started spraying the cafeteria with automatic-weapons fire. Clearly these are committed professionals and their good faith is hard to question. And when I took the test there on my back porch, groping my way from item to item, I wasn't offended once, so I guess they're doing their job. But that's a problem too. The demands the test writers must satisfy help explain why the test is so dull—all their energies have gone into bleaching their product of any conceivable provocation, rather than finding ways to make it interesting. And the pressure to please critics never ends. Long before the Americans with Disabilities Act, for instance, test preparers had accommodated people with physical disabilities: kids who couldn't use pencils or keyboards, for instance, could bring people to fill in the answer sheets for them, and blind test takers were given tests in Braille or furnished proctors who would read the test aloud. Then the question of "learning disabilities" arrived.

Beginning in the 1990s, activists demanded that students with Attention Deficit and Hyperactivity Disorder be granted extra time to complete the test, to place them on an even footing with other, less distracted test takers. The companies agreed, and the number of test takers claiming to suffer from ADHD rose dramatically. Then the test companies expressed surprise at what the data revealed a few years later: if you give some kids more time to take a test, they will get higher scores than kids who didn't get more time to take the test. So the College Board decided to "flag" these scores as a kind of caveat emptor, to alert admissions officers that the test taker, though claiming a learning disability, might have been given an unfair advantage.

Activists sued for discrimination. By flagging the scores, they said, the ETS and College Board were "stigmatizing" applicants with ADHD. After a halfhearted defense, the companies conceded the point, and flagging was discontinued. Today a kid claiming ADHD can take as much as an extra hour to finish the test.

The generous and seemingly endless concessions drew the most public attention in 1995. SAT sections are graded on a scale of 200 to 800, and average scores had been sinking since the end of the Second World War. The mean verbal score had fallen from 501 in 1941 to 425 by 1990; the mean math score dropped 502 to 475 during the same period. One possible reaction to this sorry turn might be a redoubled effort to improve the quality of secondary education, to raise the scores of kids back to the level of their grandparents. Instead, ETS "recentered" the grading system, so that a 425 on the old scale became a 501 on the new scale. Everyone was automatically smarter. It's not quite like Lake Woebegone, where all the kids are above average. But the recentering did guarantee that at least as many kids are above average today as seventy years ago.

Many of these adjustments were necessary for technical reasons or reasons of fairness, and certainly they're defensible for reasons of public perception. But in making them, the companies also inadvertently reinforced the premise of their critics. Scholastic aptitude was made to seem an arbitrary concept without grounding in anything real, a fiction subject to endless revision—something that suited the needs of one generation but was now entirely outmoded. The companies conceded the point when they agreed, in 1994, to drop the word "aptitude" from the name of their test.

It was a remarkable concession that would have floored earlier progressives like James Conant or Riesman and Jencks. They never entertained the idea that aptitude was, as one critic put it not long ago, a "tool of repression." They might have asked how it was that first-generation Asian immigrant females routinely outperformed native-born white males on a test that native-born white males had supposedly rigged for their own advantage. Those white males must not be as smart as everybody thought.

So IF TESTS NO LONGER measure aptitude, what are they for? The companies have tried to keep their claims modest. Always they have disavowed any grand intention of sorting the American population on the basis of academic ability. And in fact the only people claiming that the SAT was intended to rank people according to their worth as members of society were SAT critics like the journalists Lemann and Owen, who of course deplored the idea. The grand manifesto of FairTest is titled: "Test Scores Do Not Equal Merit." And they don't. But who said they did? Not the ETS, not the College Board, and not the dwindling number of disinterested observers who defend the central role of standardized tests in college admissions. The companies have themselves published books and studies attacking what they called the "myth of the single yardstick"—the notion that "there can be one and only one primary ordering of people as 'best qualified.'"

Instead, the College Board says that the SAT does nothing more than measure "developed critical thinking and reasoning skills needed for success in college." To judge whether it succeeds in that task, thousands of statistical and psychometric studies have been done. (The SAT is easily the most chewed-over academic work product in history.) The consensus is that SAT scores do a fairly good job of predicting what kind of grades applicants will get in their freshman year—one measure of "success in college." If you consider both their SAT scores and their high school grade-point average, you have an even better predictor of how well they'll do in the first year. These findings alone are enough to establish SAT scores as a useful piece of information for admissions officers trying to figure out if an applicant is well suited to their college. And if you're an admissions officer at a large university, trying to get a handle on twenty or thirty thousand applications, the SAT is not only useful but indispensable.

Yet because the achievement gaps persist—no amount of sensitivity tinkering has been able to close them—the calls for down-grading or eliminating the SAT persist too. And it's indeed undeniable that wealthier kids and kids whose parents went to college get better SAT scores. The law professor Lani Guinier says the SAT should therefore simply be called a "wealth test." Another activist says the test measures nothing but "the size of the student's house." "The only thing that SAT predicts well now is socioeconomic status," one University of California dean told the *L.A. Times*.

The problem for SAT critics is that the gaps show up far beyond SAT scores. My reading in the subject led me to the work of Rebecca Zwick, an education professor at the University of California Santa Barbara. (She's the one who collected the quotes above from Guinier and the others.) Zwick writes flatly that it's "impossible to find a measure of academic achievement that is unrelated to family income." Some reformers have gone full circle from Conant and suggest that scores on "achievement tests"—the kind Conant thought unfairly benefited rich boys—should replace SAT scores for use in admission. Others suggest using high school grade-point averages alone, or high school class rank. Some suggest using a composite number—compiled from high school grades, personal interviews, writing tests, the difficulty of high school course load, and extent of extracurricular activities—to replace the SAT in a school's deliberations. Test-optional colleges are all using one version or another of these alternatives.

Yet Zwick discovered that each of these markers correlates with family income as much as, and in some cases more than, the SAT. Kids who get high "aptitude" scores also get high "achievement" scores. While high school grades are a good predictor of college success for middle- and upper-income kids, the link weakens with kids from lower-income backgrounds. Wealthy kids are more likely to grow up around books, so—on average, always on average—they get better writing scores; they have more opportunity for extracurricular activities, so their résumés are fuller; their schools have deeper course offerings, so their course loads look more challenging. The rankings of kids look much the same whether they're measured by aptitude tests, achievement tests, high school grades, writing tests, the difficulty of their course loads . . . By the numbers, the bias toward the well-to-do is hard to budge.

The frustration that progressive educators feel is understandable and, given their own idealism, perfectly appropriate. But it has pushed them to embrace measures that would have been laughable even a generation ago. One statistician, writing in the *Harvard Educational Review*, has suggested that a "corrective scoring method" be applied to the SAT. Not only do different groups perform differently on the SAT, he pointed out; groups show differences in the *kinds* of SAT questions they do well on. So his R-SAT grading system would count only the questions on which those groups score well. Ta-da: "The R-SAT," he wrote, "shows an increase in SAT verbal scores by as much as 200 or 300 points for individual minority test-takers."

It's déjà vu. As Karabel showed in *The Chosen,* when the test scores didn't work out the way the blue bloods wanted back in the old days, they did the obvious thing: they played down the numbers. They went looking for personal qualities they could use in place of aptitude. And of course they found what they were looking for, in hazy notions like "good breeding," "manliness," "All-Americanness"—considerations that would yield the kind of class the old boys were comfortable with, a class with fewer undesirable elements. Nowadays, with standardized tests yielding a disproportionate number of Asians and well-to-do whites, progressives resort to an updated version of the old blue-blood technique. Only now they're using social science to lend an air of statistical precision.

The marketers at the College Board have noticed the trend. In keeping with their finely honed instinct for survival, the companies are trying to lead the parade before they get trampled. In 2008 College Board researchers announced that they would try to develop standardized tests to measure "noncognitive skills"—amorphous attributes beyond the merely intellectual, which could be linked to success in college, tested for and quantified, without resulting in a scoring gap. It goes without saying that if the College Board could develop such tests it would be happy to sell them to new generations of college goers. "If You Can't Beat 'Em, Join 'Em" read the headline in the trade publication *Inside Higher Ed*.

The CB's effort is based largely on work already done by psychologists at Michigan State University, who have devised a "12-dimension taxonomy" on which to test students. "Knowledge and mastery of general principles" is only one of the twelve. The others include "social responsibility," "interpersonal skills," "multicultural tolerance and appreciation," and "cultural appreciation and curiosity." Unfortunately, so far none of their results have been able to predict college success with anywhere near the reliability of SAT scores. Sliced another way, however, the results are quite pleasing. The CB calculated that if the twelve-dimension scores were used in college admissions at a selective college, the percentage of black students and Hispanic students admitted to the school would more than double. On the other hand, the percentage of Asians would drop by one-third. But who's counting.

An even more ambitious effort is known as the "Rainbow Project," developed by a psychologist named Robert Sternberg, formerly of Yale and now the dean of arts and sciences at Tufts University. Sternberg says he doesn't want to do away with the SAT altogether; he admits its predictive value. But he is also candidly trying to find a way to admit more African American and Hispanic applicants to selective colleges, and to do it with some kind of quantifiable support. His goal, he writes, is "the creation of standardized test measures that reduce the different outcomes between different groups as much as possible in a way that still maintains test validity." It's a kind of reverse engineering: he knows the results he wants, he just needs the right test to give them to him.

Sternberg's method is pretty straightforward. He's taken the tenderhearted and almost true bit of grandmotherly wisdom—everyone is good at something—and stretched it to the breaking point: everyone is good at something that will make him a successful college student at a selective school. This is the premise of his "triarchic theory of intelligence." Sternberg's thinking is inspired by the well-known work of the Harvard psychologist Howard Gardner, who in 1983 claimed to have identified seven kinds of human intelligence, from bodily-kinesthetic intelligence to intrapersonal intelligence; recently he discovered another intelligence, for a total of eight, though more intelligences may be on the way. Sternberg, more modest, has contented himself with only three—a trio of skills that, when quantified, should be as useful and impressive to college admissions officers as any SAT score.

Sternberg's definitions are highly abstract. *Practical intelligence* involves "skills used to implement, apply, or put into practice ideas in real-world contexts." *Creative intelligence* involves "skills used to create, invent, discover, imagine, suppose, or hypothesize." *Analytical intelligence* is closer to more conventional notions of intelligence, and to the aptitude that the SAT has typically been thought to measure. It involves "skills used to analyze, evaluate, judge, or compare and contrast."

To measure his intelligences Sternberg has developed a combination of multiple-choice tests, which resemble the SAT, and "performance measures," which do not. Together the testing session can last four hours. You can see why. If nothing else, the Rainbow test would be much livelier than the SAT. After going through an SAT-like multiple-choice section, the student is handed five cartoons from the *New Yorker* magazine and told to write a fresh caption for each. "Trained judges" (Sternberg's term) grade the captions on a five-point scale, depending on how original, clever, funny, and "task-appropriate" they are. Then the student is asked to write two stories under such provocative titles as "The Octopus's Sneakers" and "Beyond the Edge." Again trained judges are standing by to rank the responses with a number (one to five again).

Then: straight to video. The student watches seven brief vignettes about an everyday problem and chooses one out of six options for how to handle it. His answer is judged, from one to seven, on how well it would solve the problem. Then come two written questionnaires, one measuring "common sense" and another rating reactions to "college life." (Example: How would you deal with a difficult roommate?)

Finally, there's biodata—"bio" is short for biographical—in which students grade themselves on how hard they study, how hard they play, how involved they are in school. Biodata plays a crucial role in almost all noncognitive tests, as a replacement for, or a supplement to, more conventional assessments of aptitude. A typical example comes from a test developed at the University of Maryland. Students are asked to rate how strongly they agree with various statements about themselves. "Once I start something, I finish it." "I want a chance to prove myself academically." "When I believe strongly in something, I act on it." The higher the score, the more desirable the kid.

It's odd—more, it's hard to believe—that noncognitive tests such as these are being floated to rival a test, the SAT, which is routinely deemed defective because it is too subjective, too coachable, too imprecise, too clumsy to administer, and too dependent on cultural conventions. What, after all, could be more subjective than rating the humor in the captions of *New Yorker* cartoons, assuming you could find any? What's more coachable than asking a kid whether he finishes what he starts? (If he leaves the question blank, you've got your answer.) It only makes sense when you remember that the point of the new tests is not their objectivity or precision but the scores that they elicit, particularly from individuals lashed together by race, sex, or income level. Sternberg says he can claim some success in this regard. "Although the group differences in the tests were not reduced to zero," he writes, "the tests did substantially attenuate group differences relative to other measures such as the SAT." Interest in Sternberg's method among admissions officers has been intense.

Anyone who drifts unprepared into psychometric literature will be surprised to discover the platitudes that rise like air sanitizer from even the most impenetrable studies. Huge stretches of Sternberg's work are virtually unintelligible to a layman like me (worse than the word problems on the SAT: "A chi-squared test for differences between sample variance and population variance suggests that variance for the sample for these items . . ."). And then suddenly you trip over a sentence that might have come from "The Uncollected Polonius": "Success in life requires one not only to analyze one's own ideas as well as the ideas of others, but also to generate ideas and persuade other people of their value." If Polonius had a master's degree in sociology: "A balance of skills is needed to adapt to, shape, and select environments."

But platitudes—truisms—are everywhere in the anti-SAT literature. Truisms lull the reader so reassuringly that you might miss other stuff that isn't true at all. Martha Allman, Wake Forest's admissions director, announced the school's decision to drop their SAT requirement with self-flattering banalities. "After months of discussion and study and reflection," she said, "we decided it was time to stand up on the side of fairness." Meanwhile, the material Wake Forest issued to support its new test-optional policy contained a series of statements that are demonstrably untrue: that SATs aren't good predictors of college success, that they're merely an indicator of socioeconomic status rather than aptitude, that they're a barrier to college for "many well-qualified students," that they're crippled with cultural and racial bias, that their "coachability" renders them useless, and so on. Each of these is contradicted by mountains of data and common sense.

There are also mountains of data that call into question the process that testing-optional colleges use when they dismiss the SAT. Wake Forest officials said they'd rely more heavily on "achievement outside the classroom," the rigor of the applicant's high school course load, achievement-test scores, and personal interviews conducted either on campus, over Skype, or by a far-flung network of alumni. But as Rebecca Zwick and other researchers point out, each of these gives the well-to-do an obvious advantage too. Even personal interviews: given the larger range of social inter-action their backgrounds have afforded them, middle- and upper-class kids are also more likely to handle personal interviews calmly and with élan. Unavoidably, on-campus interviews with profes-sional counselors will count for more than those conducted over the Internet or with half-trained alum volunteers. And only the better-off students will be able to spare the time and expense to travel to Wake Forest for an admissions interview.

No matter which way they turn, progressive admissions offi-cials are thrown back on the hard truth that Jencks and Riesman pointed out: life is unfair to the poor, and one sign of its unfairness is that it offers them fewer chances to develop the skills that col-leges and universities have traditionally rewarded—the skills that admissions officers have traditionally sought out and that the SAT measures. No less than Conant seventy years ago, however, col-lege educators are moved by a reformist impulse to right society's wrongs. It's just that the character of their idealism has changed as the country has changed. Progressives of Conant's era would have said fairness lies in treating everyone equally by giving them access to the same objective test. For today's progressives—the kind who staff most admissions offices—fairness lies in ignoring the test alto-gether, if it fails to yield the results you've already decided are fair. The SAT and its reputation are victims of this newer progressivism. I'm not sure the schools are its beneficiaries.

IN THE DAY-TO-DAY LIFE OF the college applicant, particularly one whose family has been seized by admissions anxiety, the SAT has lost none of its power. It looms. It enthralls. More than 1.5 mil-lion kids take it each year. High school counselors build curricu-lums around it. The test-prep business continues to boom. Kaplan is the sole profit center of its corporate parent, the Washington Post Company. If you can afford to keep a metropolitan newspaper afloat, you're making a lot of money.

The most my son got from Kaplan, as far as I could tell, was the test booklet I struggled over on the back porch that spring morning. At the beginning of their course he took a test. After ten weeks of classroom sessions two nights a week, he took another. The difference in scores was negligible. He would have done the same with a few concentrated reviews of math and vocabulary, using material available for free at school or on the Web. The experience did instill him with a reverential awe of the SAT, which the Kaplan company must know is good for business. Most sectors of the college admissions economy are still heavily invested in the mystique of standardized testing.

Thanks to the dishwashing, coffeemaking, dog walking, and sports-page reading I'd indulged in to stretch the breaks and try to recharge my brain, I finished my own test session past lunchtime. I got through the ten sections in about four and a half hours—well over my allotted three hours and forty-five minutes. By then my son had returned from taking the test at the high school.

"Hard," was all he said when I asked him how the SAT had gone.

"No kidding," I said. After he'd eaten a couple of hot dogs—this took thirty seconds—I enlisted him to help me score my test. From the key provided he read the correct answers while I scanned my little ovals, which I had filled in darkly and completely—very darkly and very completely but, it was soon apparent, not very correctly. There were moments, grading the math sections, when I thought he might be putting me on. Section 9, a series of algebraic problems, consisted of sixteen questions; in twenty minutes I had managed to answer twelve of them and got eleven of them wrong.

"Wow," he said. "That's like, what, eight percent correct?"

"How would I know?" I said, testy. "I can't do percentages."

"Obviously."

I used his calculator to compute my raw score onto the SAT scale of 200 to 800. My critical reading score was okay—pretty damn good, in fact. The math score . . . I'm not giving my math score. It was low enough to take your breath away, however—a level somewhere below "lobotomy patient" but above "Phillies fan." Scoring the essay on the suggested one-to-six scale was trickier. College Board guidelines say that for an essay to receive the highest score, it must show "clear coherence and smooth progression of ideas" (what's unclear coherence?), "skillful use of language," "effectively and insightfully develop a point of view," and "use clearly appropriate examples."

A fitting description of my essay, I thought. It had clearly earned a six, but I knocked a point off for modesty's sake. Even with the strong essay score, my SATs were close to a disaster, as they had been thirty-five years ago, when the grass trimmings drifting through the window had at least given me a plausible excuse.

My son read the essay to confirm my score. I tried not to watch him as he read.

"Three," he said at last.

"Three?"

"Maybe two."

"Come on. Two?"

"Okay, four."

"You're crazy."

"Read the guidelines," he said. "Read the prep booklets. They all say the same thing. You need three supporting examples. You've got that one thing about the First World War. And you jump around a lot."

"That's juxtaposition," I said. "I wanted to introduce some complexity."

"And you end with a question. 'Where do little acorns come from?' Why would you end with a question? You're supposed to be making a point."

I could see he was trying to be gentle but having trouble.

"I'm sure that's okay for a magazine or a book," he went on. "But this is the SAT. You can't get away with that stuff on the SAT."

5

MAKING THE SALE

Kitchen People—the collapsing mom—excellent odds—
from here to anywhere—the high and the low—
Tulane's brand—a dream tour—
Harvard and freemasons—Dartmouth and dental dams

WHEN THEY popped into his e-mail queue a few weeks later, his scores were good—better than mine, for what it's worth. They were good enough anyway not to require serious revisions to the early list of schools he was mentally compiling: the safeties were still a decent bet, the reach schools were still a reach. At the same time, a new element of competition was added to the kitchen palavers I found myself engaging in most weekends. These were parties within parties, small clusters of parents of college-age kids that detached themselves from the larger group of suburban couples on a Saturday night or Sunday afternoon, drawn together to the kitchen or back deck like newborn hamsters huddling in a corner of the cage. We were Kitchen People. We craved companionship and comfort, exchanged gossip, news, questions, and complaints, sought solace, advice, and a chance to spy on the competition.

The arrival of the SAT scores opened up new possibilities for palaver. A few of us treated our kids' GPAs and SATs the way we'd treat our salary or the price we paid for our house, as something not to be surrendered in general conversation, on grounds of privacy and taste. It would make you look like a braggart—or a loser, depending on the numbers involved. Others were less delicate. The weekend would come, and in the kitchen, in the reflected shimmer from the brushed-steel doors of the Sub-Zero, the subtle dance would begin.

"Well," one mother might say of her daughter, "she's not even going to bother to apply to Princeton, not now, not with those SATs. It'd just be crazy now."

"That bad, eh," another parent would say, feigning sympathy.

"I mean, don't get me wrong," the mother would hurriedly interject, as if correcting herself. "Her SATs are fine, very solid. Just not in Princeton territory. That's all I meant. She'd be right on the cusp, probably. Kind of marginal. You know, it's not out of the question. Maybe she'll apply. Don't know. It's not like it would be crazy or anything."

There were dour parents too, ground down from years of unfulfilled expectations, by dashed paternal hopes and the less-than-stellar performance of their children. They would volunteer their children's scores slowly, first math, then verbal, then writing, in prolonged self-flagellation.

"He's a smart kid," the dad would say, "I guess. But his scores are just terrible. He doesn't work at it. I've tried. We got him a Kaplan book. I offered to pay for the course. He'd rather play video games. Can you major in video games at college these days? He's a standout if you can. Magna cum laude in Grand Theft Auto IV."

Others whose children scored in the stratosphere could be caught squirming against the Viking oven, sometimes literally hopping up and down, gently at first but unmistakably, not wanting to brag or anything or seem impolite but . . . *jeezus* . . . they were just going to explode if they didn't tell you how their daughter had brought home a 2400, perfect in every test—and together with her GPA was now destined for the sunlit uplands of Dartmouth or

Brown, perhaps (though it's too much to say out loud) even HYP: Harvard, Yale, or Princeton. In such cases it was satisfying to let the parents squirm.

"We were really surprised at how well she did," the mother would say, running a finger around the rim of her glass of pink Zinfandel. Her eyes plead, *Ask me what they were, just please please ask . . .*

"Oh?" I'd say.

"Her father was like, Oh, My, God." She'd be twisting a foot inward now and bending slightly at the knees, as though seized with an urge to pee. And from the eyes, silently: *Ask.*

"Mmm," I'd say.

"Of course, she's always been a smart kid"—bending lower, lower—"brighter than her mom, that's for sure! My scores when I took the SAT twenty-five years ago—they were nothing like hers."

"Mmm."

"Of course, she tests well in general, always has. But scores like these . . ." Her pride bladder was terribly distended now, swelling in all directions, thumping up against the anterior walls of the pelvis, pressing down into the pubic bone, squeezing the hypogastric artery, this painful unsatisfied need driving her nearly to the slate flooring . . .

"I mean when the e-mail with the scores arrived, I just had to peek!" She cast her pleading eyes around the kitchen for other parents who might be listening. "And then when I did, I'm thinking, 'My God—this is *my* kid? Where'd those scores come from?'"

At last she'd catch a sympathetic eye, and another parent would say, "They must have been really—"

"Twenty-four hundred! I'm like, Wow!"

And then, having passed the stone, she'd stand up straight as a barge pole, the pain suddenly gone, and sip the Zin with a humble smile.

I WAS BECOMING MORE AWARE of how colleges make themselves known to students. Snail mail was the most obvious method, enveloping the house in a mud slide of pamphlets, viewbooks, and invitations to local college nights. Just as many solicitations, or maybe more, arrived in my son's e-mail box, sometimes three or four a day, he told me, but these were less bothersome and no more revealing than what the mailman brought. Whether in digital or paper form, they left little impression on him that I could see.

"Why do they send me these things?" he asked (rhetorically) one day, waving a come-on from the University of Miami.

I told him it must be full of cleverly subliminal signals designed to make him want to catch the next plane for Florida. The face of the card was stamped WE WANT TO GET TO KNOW YOU over a picture of students lounging on sun-warmed grass, a fountain playing amid hints of bougainvillea and birds of paradise. I held up the card.

"What is this saying to you?"

"They want to get to know me," he said.

I told him to look more closely.

"It's sunny," he said. "Springtime. Kind of pretty."

"Closer. Look at the students."

"They look happy."

"Yeah," I said.

"There's only one guy," he said. "Surrounded by girls. Four girls."

"And what's that say to you?"

"It says, 'Excellent odds.'"

"See? They're trying to manipulate you. It's a very subtle message: if you come here, you can take your pick."

"Dad," he said, suddenly serious. "I've been thinking. I don't know why, but I really want to go to the University of Miami."

The sophistication with which the schools present themselves to the world, and to their potential students, is a relatively recent development. Higher education, I'd already learned, is a highly competitive industry in which the competitors have tried not to look (1) competitive or (2) like an industry. As recently as twenty years ago it was uncommon for admissions officers even to use the vulgar word "marketing." And then in 2008, a survey reported that the most important qualification in hiring a dean of admissions was a "background in marketing/public relations."

The demographic scare of the late seventies, when college deans worried they might soon run out of customers, made this happen. First the educators-turned-marketers had to identify their customer base (they were soon to begin using terms like "customer base"). They found the data readily at hand. Since the early 1970s, the College Board has included a Student Descriptive Questionnaire in the PSAT. Most students who take the test also take the time to fill out the questionnaire. This gives the CB a comprehensive list of the kids who want to go to college that year, along with lots of information about each. They give up their address, GPA, ethnicity, academic interests, and extracurricular activities. They estimate family income and disclose whether they expect to request financial aid. ACT, the SAT rival which tests kids mostly in the Midwest, collects similar information. Two for-profit firms have entered the list-compiling business too; they get their information by mailing millions of questionnaires to high school teachers for distribution to their students.

Together, these four lists yield a mother lode of data about nearly every college-bound high school student in the United States. Marketers in other industries can only gasp in envy. Imagine if you had a list of everybody in the country who planned to buy a car in the next twelve months, along with their addresses, income, and preferences in color, style, size, seat covers, sound systems, gas mileage—you would be able to make many car salesmen very happy, for a fee. And that's what the list companies offer the country's colleges and universities.

For a fee—roughly thirty cents per student name—schools hire the companies to search their lists for students who fit a desired profile. The search criteria vary from school to school, of course. Admissions deans have identified more flavors of American youth than Baskin-Robbins has discovered in a half-century of making ice cream: first-generation Hispanic boys with a gift for basketball and critical writing, wealthy African American girls with an interest in physics and a commitment to community service, religious Anglos of whatever sex from the Southeast with strong math scores and a hankering to study abroad.

Not all searches need to be esoteric. An Ivy League school will search for the A-plus students with high test scores, and then cull the list by region, career plans, and half a dozen other factors: they'll search only for high-scoring kids who want to go to four-year colleges, for example—no point for Brown to bother a brilliant student who's intent on getting a cosmetician's license.

Montana State might want to search for kids with a B average or above who love winter sports. (Sound reasoning: Why else would a Sunbelt kid want to go to school in Montana, if not to snow-board? Horses, maybe—so there's a search for kids with an interest in equinology too.) A liberal arts school with no facilities for training hard scientists will want high schoolers with high verbal scores, and they'll ignore math scores. A small Baptist college unlikely to draw kids from across the country buys the name of every college-bound Baptist within two hundred miles of campus.

An admissions dean can slice the salami very thin indeed, exploring even questions of personal disposition. One questionnaire asks students their preference in "campus environment." They can check off "conservative" (a campus that enforces strict bans on drugs or alcohol) or "moderate" (where "reasonable behavioral norms" are observed), or "liberal" (pass the bong). A Christian college like Pepperdine will want to buy names from the first group of students, an experimental college like Reed will buy kids in the third.

The competition for names has grown so intense that schools are now doing something they would never have done ten years ago—buying the names of high school sophomores. These doe-eyed innocents were long thought to be too changeable, too unformed in their preferences, to respond reliably to even the most sophisticated targeting. Some deans, slightly appalled, call it "search creep," others call it cradle-robbing; most of them do it anyway. No one knows how young the searches will eventually go. Kat Cohen's daughter in pre-K might want to check her e-mail. A successful college is first at everything: first to search the right names and buy them, first to hit the kids with a viewbook, first to invite them to campus, first to mail them an application, first to notify them of an acceptance, first to make them a tuition offer they can't refuse.

A LARGE, LUCRATIVE, AND PARASITIC industry has puckered up and suctioned itself onto the tumescent host of college admissions. Copywriters, graphic designers, demographers, event planners, statistical researchers, photographers, even color specialists counsel the admissions committees on what to mail and when. As the attention span of kids shrinks along with their tolerance for the written word, mottos and slogans have become increasingly important—and expensive. Hundreds of thousands of dollars are spent each year on professionals who are presumed to be gifted at writing the perfect pithy five or six words that will convey a school's essence to the world.

I'd seen examples in the *U.S. News* special issue—"The Character of Success." Or "The Success of Character." I'd forgotten already. Long ago, a portentous Latin phrase was sufficient. Yale committed itself to *Lux et Veritas*, Light and Truth; Northwestern pursued *Quaecumque sunt vera*, Whatsoever things are true. These are phrases that not many college graduates would even try to pronounce here in the twenty-first century, and the post-postmodern age has rendered all those claims about Truth highly suspect. So today's school mottoes follow the same rudimentary principles that songwriters used in choosing song titles in the early days of rock and roll, the first mass commercial enterprise targeted exclusively at teenagers. A good title used simple words, a personal pronoun or two, and present-tense verbs to convey a sense of immediacy and belonging: "She Loves You," "Baby It's You," "Be My Baby" "You Baby," classics all.

And so it is with recent college mottoes, like Olivet University's "We Believe You Belong Here, Baby" (I added the "Baby"), "Where You Belong" (Barry University), "Where Are You Going?" (Bethany College), "Where Everybody Is Somebody" (Howard Payne University), "This Is the Place" (Texas A&M). Sometimes the mottoes are too cute ("Changing Futures by Degrees," University of Houston), sometimes too enigmatic and brooding ("What Really Matters?," University of Dubuque). But none is written in stone. Colleges buy mottoes and try them on and cast them off as if they were sizing up costume jewelry.

A few years ago, the University of Idaho was happy with "From Here You Can Go Anywhere." Then it became clear that many other schools were making the same boast. Variants of "Start Here, Go Anywhere" were in use from Belmont University in Tennessee to Emporia State University in Kansas, from Massachusetts Bay College to Gulf Coast College—a geographic variety that did suggest, contrary to the motto, that you could start here, there, or everywhere and still go anywhere. After much expense, Idaho settled on "Open Spaces, Open Minds," but only temporarily. The last I looked, the school had left the Open Spaces for "A Legacy of Leading."

"WHAT WE DO IS A mixture of the high and the low," an admissions officer once told me. "We really do care about these kids, we really do. How could we not? We're in the business of developing young minds, nurturing spirits—all that.

"On the other hand," she continued, "we're marketers. We really do want to make the sale."

Unlike many of her peers, she herself revels without scruple in the commercial tricks of modern admissions. She held up a viewbook and explained how it worked. I would never have dreamed that so much care and ingenuity lay behind the large, flopping folios of stapled paper that had been cascading into my house for months. As a senior in high school, in the mid-1970s, I sent off a request for information to Occidental College, the school that would become my alma mater. A week later a thick catalog arrived in the mail. Page after cream-colored page was dense with type: course descriptions, personal testimonials, departmental mission statements, financial information, and biographical notes on eminent professors. A few smudged black-and-white photos of students riding bikes and hoisting backpacks were the only concession to atmospherics. Today such a booklet would act on the minds of high schoolers like the swaying timepiece of a hypnotist: sleepy, sleepy, and zzzzzzzz in ten seconds. That's what it did to me, in 1974.

Today's viewbooks, she said, were the perfect symbol of the change that admissions had undergone over the last thirty years. Now it's all about building a brand.

What's a brand? she asked. It's a message architecture, she said, that gives consistency to the mental impression an admissions committee wants to develop in the mind of a young person. And how do you build a brand? With color and images, not with words—though typefaces can serve as visual cues. Rip a page from a viewbook, any page, and you should still be able to identify the viewbook it came from—and the school that produced the viewbook. Color palette is key, she said. Choose carefully! If you've picked lime green for your viewbook, your Web site—lime green is an increasingly popular color, she insisted when I balked, lime green says promise, it says youth—then your Web site had better have lime green too. Respect your color palette. A lime-green school can't just run out and become a purple school over a weekend.

Each page of the viewbook is the same, but each page is different, because each page adds a new layer of information in the same style as the page before it: a page for dorm life, a page for study abroad, a page about your surrounding community. And every page has to have a "call to action." Call this toll-free number. Visit our Web site. Come to these special events. Get the kids invested, keep them turning the page.

Talk about benefits, not features; talk about the kid, not the school. Address them directly. Don't brag about your ten-to-one faculty student ratio. Say: our amazingly low faculty-to-student ratio gives you more opportunities for original research! Don't talk about class size. Say: our intimate classroom environment will better position you for graduate work! Don't say our million-book library is big and new. Say: our state-of-the-art information retrieval system will prepare you for the challenges of the twenty-first-century workplace!

Make them think they're about to get something for free: send in this card so we can send you our new brochure: "The Ten Secrets the Admissions Deans Don't Want You to Hear." Everybody likes secrets. And they like pictures. Photographs are like colors—choose carefully. Back in the day every viewbook had a "Three in a Tree": two girls and one boy, or two boys and one girl—depending on your audience—sitting on the branches of an old oak in the quad. Too dull. Now you keep your photographers on call. If there's a lovely snowfall one morning, or spectacular fall foliage, they get the call and you get the picture. Show kids looking straight at the camera—it draws the reader in. You want a sense of sociability and participation. Students in groups! Working together! Lots of smiles! This place is fun! Every photo tells the story of your institution. If you're up to your neck in science majors and want some arty types, get a photo of the pretty girl at a pottery wheel. If you need boys, get an action picture of the football team. Hopefully in the mud. Boys like mud.

And if you think you need to give out information in the viewbook, okay. Remember, though, information has to come in nuggets. Try a list of numbers: number of our Fulbright scholars since 2003: ten! Number of swimming pools on campus: six! Number of hours our food service is open: twenty-four! Like that.

Branding requires discipline, and discipline starts in your office. Ask your staff, If your school were a car, what would it be? A Mercedes, a Yugo, a Jeep? Schools in a rural setting might want to be a Ford Explorer: rugged, practical, earthy. A very selective, very expensive school—a Juilliard, a Curtis—might think of itself as a Lamborghini: exclusive, exquisite, high-class, and high-maintenance. Get the office talking. If one of your associate deans says the school is a Lexus and the other says it's a Chevy truck—you've got a problem.

And one last point: play to your strengths. It sounds obvious, right? A lot of obvious things never register, especially with deans and professors and other people who never quite get it. So tell them about Tulane.

This was before Katrina, of course. Tulane was underperforming for years because it didn't play to its strengths. The only thing the viewbooks talked about was academics: kids in the library, kids in the lab. All the deans and professors insisted on it. They said, We already have a rep as a party school, let's stress our great academics.

Right. Snooze. Surprise, surprise: apps down, SATs down, tuition revenue down.

A new dean brought in a branding agency. They did the focus groups—college students, applicants, high school students. And it jumped right out at them: Excuse me, we're in freakin' New Orleans! They cooked up a viewbook with Mardi Gras colors, lots of New Orleans, rich cultural heritage, diversity, gumbo, streetcars, jazz, the Quarter at night . . . and response went straight up. You could chart it on a graph, like a hockey stick. Same search, same kind of names. But different brand.

Response rate, up. Yield, up. SAT scores, up. GPAs, up. More kids from the top 10 percent of their class than ever before. They're climbing the page at *U.S. News.* And the number of full-pays, the kids who don't need aid: way, way up.

Why? A lotta rich kids think it'd be neat to live in New Orleans. Mom and dad will pay for it if they think it's about college, even if the kids know different. Being a good school wasn't enough. Being a good school *in New Orleans*—now you can make a sale.

ADMISSIONS OFFICERS SPEND LOTS OF time on the road, visiting high schools, attending college fairs, and holding events of their own— college nights—to spread the word and bring the customers into the tent. Twenty years ago admissions committees would promote their traveling shows by sending a schedule to each of the names they'd bought—usually a single card listing all their events across the country—regardless of where they lived.

The technique seems impossibly crude today. Targeted students now receive individual invitations for the event in their area, slipped in an envelope with an RSVP card, as if they were being asked to a dinner dance at the club. The invitation describes the event as an opportunity—not merely to learn about the school but also to meet future students, local alumni, and the admissions officer for their region, who will after all be reading their app. Perhaps even the dean himself! The RSVP card is essential, studies show: it can create a sense of obligation in the recipients, especially kids who've never been flattered to receive one before. They feel bad if they don't fill it out, and obliged to go if they do.

It certainly worked in our case, for a while. We were at our fourth college night when I realized that the law of diminishing returns had set in. Like the other information sessions we'd been to, it was held on a weeknight in the grand ballroom of an exurban hotel. In new hotels "grand ballroom" is a misnomer. They're just basements in disguise: you enter the hotel from the parking lot and instead of going up you go down, riding the escalators back and forth and down and down to a vast room where the shimmering chandeliers, the movable walls in gilded trim, and the richly patterned carpet give off miscues of Vegas opulence. The illusion never holds for long. With the low ceilings running the length of a football field, and the chilled, pumped-in air, and the hum and rumble from the boiler room just beyond the fire door, you can't forget where you really are, which is in a very shiny cellar.

It's a strange setting for a higher-education event, but again it's a mix of the high and the low, as if Donald Trump had decided to sponsor a chamber music festival. On this night the turnout made the big space necessary. A thousand kids or more had been chauffeured in by their parents from every corner of suburbia. Among the host schools were Princeton and Harvard. Their presence explained the crowd. For unknowable reasons the two Ivies had condescended to let BSU, our flagship state school, join them for college night—whether out of deference to the locals or as a gesture of noblesse oblige, I couldn't guess.

We were there for BSU. The boy had just come off a sleepless week of spring finals, and the only way I'd been able to persuade him to come, the only reason I wanted to come myself, was the promise of meeting BSU's admissions officer and making a benign and enduring impression on him. At the very least, I said, he could leave his name on the sign-up sheets that were always available at such events. Over and over again I'd heard that any proof of curiosity or interest—like a visit to an info session—would wind up in an applicant's file and be a mark in his favor. Admissions committees like an applicant who likes them.

In the hall outside the ballroom we worked our way through the crowd to the host tables. With a turnout this size, my son said, there'd be no chance to suck up to the BSU dean. And when we got to the tables there were no sign-up sheets, no greeters from the admissions offices; only teetering stacks of viewbooks, looking orphaned.

He shrugged. "Nowhere to sign in," he said. "They'll never

even know we were here. It's pointless." He turned back toward the escalators. "We might as well go home, right? Okay?"

We took seats close to the front of the ballroom. The deans were seated on a stage in easy chairs, flanked by end tables and lit with lamps shaped like the one that got Aladdin into so much trouble. A large screen for the PowerPoint was hung behind them. The crowd was unusually quiet, I thought, though many of the parents had that overeager look, as if they might storm the stage and grab the lamps and start rubbing them. Others looked more detached, moms fresh from the office, dads in dress slacks and loosened ties and rolled-up shirtsleeves, thumbing their BlackBerries and scrolling through e-mail, keeping contact with the world they preferred to this one, filled with other people's kids.

"I hate these things," my son said. "It's not good for my self-esteem. Everyone here is smarter than me."

"Oh, bull," I said. "How can you tell?"

"You can just tell." He nodded toward a kid across the aisle who looked like Jerry Lewis in *The Nutty Professor*.

"Well, that kid, maybe," I said. "But not the others, necessarily."

I noticed he had put on his BSU sweatshirt. He was craftier than he appeared—why was I still surprised every time I rediscovered this? Maybe because my surprise always faded so quickly: he pulled out a magazine, opened it in his lap, and began reading.

"You're reading *Mad* magazine?"

"No, I'm just staring at it," he said. "Yes, I'm reading it."

"What if somebody sees you?" The stage where the deans sat was twenty feet away. "If you want them to think that everybody here's smarter than you, you're making an excellent case."

He ignored me and lost himself in an absorbing parody of *Deal or No Deal*. I leafed through the viewbooks, with sinking hopes. The top 25 percent of Princeton's incoming class scored 790 or 800 on their SAT verbal test. I elbowed him and ran my finger under the statistic.

"Guess I won't be applying to old Princeton," he said.

By the time the presentations began he had turned to another parody, this one about Bill O'Reilly, and was trying hard not to snort. Harvard's dean went first, then Princeton's.

"How many times have we heard all this before?" my son said, looking up.

The three college nights we'd been too had each showcased three schools.

"Nine," I said. We could have ticked off the talking points in our sleep (literally, as it happened). Vast libraries, vigorous athletics, enlightening study abroad; hundreds of clubs, heaps of organic food, dorms that were cozy in winter and airy with the fragrant breath of spring. Why, here at——, professors practically compelled students to share in their Nobel-winning research. With a one-to-one faculty ratio, average class size was infinitesimal; indeed, so small that sometimes a student might find himself in a classroom all alone! Slide shows clicked through images of leafy quads and packed stadiums, male dancers on tiptoe and women in lab coats and goggles. Hadn't we seen these same pictures at the Penn college night? And then Stanford's? Every private college in America had hired the same photo agency.

After the Ivies were done, the dean from BSU rose to speak, looking a little overwhelmed.

"If you'd told me ten years ago I'd be up here on the stage with Harvard and Princeton . . ." He let his voice trail off. He had trouble matching the Ivies boast for boast. Where they had bragged of their campuses abroad—Tuscany, if I remember, and Kensington Gardens—he mentioned the possibility of a semester on the Chesapeake Bay, not far from Rehoboth Beach, Delaware. Harvard and Princeton each said they had four hundred student clubs and organizations; BSU had three hundred. Instead of the financial aid that only an Ivy endowment makes possible—the deans said they'd cut tuition drastically for families earning up to $200,000 a year— he pointed out that BSU's state-subsidized tuition price made it competitive even without grants, which he couldn't offer anyway. As for class size, well, "Eighty-five percent of our classes are under fifty students."

Food and dorm life? a parent asked.

"We're a state school," he said, "it's not the Ritz." He looked at his feet. "The food—it's school food. And your dorm room, probably it'll just be four concrete walls and a roommate."

I elbowed my son to share amazement at the dean's candor, but he didn't respond. He was asleep.

But it somehow seemed more than mere sleep. It was a cataleptic kind of sleep, a total withdrawal of sentience—head rolling, comatose, adenoid exposing. We were close enough to the stage that I felt a knot in my stomach, a hint of panic. He was still upright but barely. I glanced backward, across the rows of young, upturned faces. They were watchful, alert. No one else was asleep. The parents directly in front of us were hunched over, squinting into the bright screens of their BlackBerries, so my son stuck up like a radio tower. I poked him again and got no response. I poked him again. "What?" he said, too loudly. The BSU dean had retaken his seat. "What?" my son said again. Onstage the dean swiveled his head toward us and stared, and I imagined him as one of the pod people in *Invasion of the Body Snatchers*, fingering the last human on the planet with a goggle-eyed look of horror.

I was sure I felt his eyes following us as I hustled the boy toward the ballroom doors.

"This is the last one of these I go to," he said, mounting the escalator, and I assured him he was correct.

THE SEASON OF SALESMANSHIP DIDN'T end with our final college night, of course. We had yet to take a college tour. We kept pushing it off. At the end of spring we attended a friend's birthday party and I wound up as ever with the Kitchen People. I met a father who had just brought his son home from their third college tour together. His son was the same age as mine. I marveled at the man's industry. During winter vacation, he told me, he had subjected his son to a long, searching interview, which he, the father, distilled into a list of interests and preferences. He submitted the list to the boy for possible revision and ultimate approval.

"I didn't want to seem too bossy," he said. "It's his future."

With the list in hand the father hit The Books, selected appropriate schools, pored over maps, and concluded that three tours by car would be necessary for his son to gather impressions of the schools that would fit the profile. Knowing the boy's preferred areas of study, he went online to read course catalogs. After picking classes, he e-mailed the professors, asking for permission to sit in.

"If I'd left it up to him we never would have gotten out of the driveway," he said. By the end of his process he had compiled a thick itinerary for each trip: information sessions, campus tours, meals at typical college hangouts, and, of course, the classes themselves. Unscheduled downtime could be filled with visits to the professors' offices.

"And now, we get back last week, and he's saying he thinks he might want to take a year off," the man said. "I don't think so. The way I see it, our children's future is too important to be left to our children."

When summer came and my son's school let out, we could no longer ignore our college tours, and the specter of this tireless, meticulous Kitchen Dad clanked around me like Marley's ghost. It was my own fault that I kept running into these people. There was something in the college search that exposed fault lines in parents that were better left submerged. I doubted whether any parent in the country worried about, obsessed over, or ruminated upon the mysteries of college admissions more than I, but scarcely a month went by that I didn't encounter a take-charge parent who was more organized, more knowledgeable, or otherwise more on the ball. Were they more invested in their children than I was in mine, were they more conscientious, or were they just crazier?

Whether from laziness or high-mindedness, I couldn't bring myself to emulate the Kitchen Dad. Instead I managed to piggy-back the college tours onto trips that were already in train, a visit to friends in New England, a wedding in Chicago, and a business trip to California. On occasional weekends we resolved to make day trips to colleges closer to home. I'd hoped we could knock off fifteen schools. We stopped after ten, when they began to melt together.

The format of the tours was unvarying, and memories of them float back to me as from a dream. At the parking lot for campus visitors, an octogenarian in a policeman's hat waves us through the gates. This is our introduction to campus security. We find our way to the admissions office by following clusters of people who are our doppelgängers: a father looking peeved, a mother looking game, and, far behind, a teenager or two lost in the faraway world of iPod and texting. More doppelgängers await us at the admissions office. The office is housed in the handsomest building at the center of campus, pointed brick or limestone or all-American clapboard with a wide and welcoming porch, dating from the earliest days of the school. With much prompting, sometimes a discreet shove, the kids approach the desk and sign in.

In time we're shuffled to a room designed to seat fifteen fewer people than the number of people who are trying to find a seat. Through the dreamy mists I see an overhead projector, but that can't be right, can it? Overhead projectors mean stern lectures from my own school days, lectures about things I don't understand. No, it must be a laptop, wedged open on a desk before a screen, poised to launch at the tap of a key a slide show and a PowerPoint. An admissions officer appears, accompanied by a pair of students, a boy and a girl, and the presentations begin: On your transcript what we look at most closely is your courses; we want to see whether the student has challenged themself. There are questions from parents: Do you accept weighted or unweighted grade-point averages? How much credit for high school Advanced Placement courses? A side door opens, and a chorus line of student guides enters. They introduce themselves, one by one, in an atmosphere of general and unaccountable hilarity. Our large group breaks into smaller groups, and the walking tour begins.

They are very lively people, these guides, an animated scrum of winks and grins. The admissions trade attracts cheerful, sociable young people. Parents pass time exchanging theories of why this is invariably so. Admissions is a job for marketers and salesmen, as we're discovering, and salesmen share the cheerful gene. Then too, a bubbly personality fortifies them against the heartbreak that comes every spring when they destroy the dearly held dreams of thousands of starry-eyed young people; it can be years before the job leaches the last drop of endorphins from the admissions professional. It's also true that when the phone rings in an admissions office it is probably a person, often a parent, consumed by grief, panic, or anger. The ability to sound like Rachael Ray at such moments is invaluable.

"Our guides are not scripted," the admissions dean will call out as our guides, doing a little Snoopy dance, lead us away. "So feel free to ask them anything—anything at all!"

But of course they don't need a script. The guides do not need to be told that as they lead their shuffling troops their first joke will be about walking backward. Backward is the way the guides walk; "engaging the tour" is called this technique. "Kids, please don't try this at home," one will say. "I'm sure the moms here will warn me if I'm about to walk off a ledge!" another will offer. "Don't worry, folks," goes another. "I've got eyes in the back of my head—I guess I need a haircut!"

There are more than 500—250—475 student clubs and organizations on campus. At least one of these is eccentric, ironic, or tongue-in-cheek: the Disciples of Bob Barker, an Iggy Stooge Marching and Chowder Society, or the Montgomery Burns Fan Club. We have twelve, seventeen, or thirteen a cappella groups, more than at any other school. But if you can't find a group that's right for you, write up a proposal, bring it to Student Services, and you can get it funded within a week. It really is that simple. "If you can't find it, found it" is more than a slogan here.

There's lots to do on campus—sometimes too much! The union shows first-run movies on weekends, and our theater arts department is ranked one of the top five in the nation. How many of you guys are thinking about theater arts? That's great. Martin Scorsese or J. J. Abrams or Wes Anderson spoke at the film school or a drama class or the arts festival a couple years ago and said he couldn't believe how incredible it was.

The parties are awesome, if that's what you're into—and this *is* college. The drinking age is twenty-one in this state, and at this school we take the law very seriously. But we also know that students are students. What it comes down to is, it's really a matter of judgment. Use good judgment and you'll be fine. That's the blue light system you're looking at there. No matter where you are you're never more than thirty yards from a blue light call box. Security is the number one priority on campus. We take security very seriously. You're studying late at the library, call security, they'll be happy to walk you back to your dorm. Campus bus runs till two a.m. on the weekends.

A Harry Potter reference is inserted here. Either the Old Dining Hall looks like Hogwarts, or the freshman class voted last year to divide themselves up into clans, or the university is hosting its annual Quidditch match this fall, or the chair of the sociology department is teaching a seminar on "Voldemort and Differentiation in Imperialist Identities." That's my roommate over there, how's it going. He's premed. We have more than 212 possible majors, but you're always free to make your own, as long as it's approved by a department head, your academic adviser, and the dean of students. They say there's a core curriculum, but it's really loose. I took pet psychology and satisfied my natural sciences requirement. My best friend's brother graduated with a degree in comparative lit and he didn't have to do any Shakespeare. His dad's like, What?

There are twenty-six, nineteen, or thirty-eight club sports available and most of them are nationally ranked. The gym is awesome. They just put that climbing wall in last year, and the Jacuzzi, you can't see it from here, is the largest in the Midwest, the South, or the Mountain States. That's the dining room where the football team eats. I'm sorry—you can't go in there. Sir, you can't go in there. The quarterback or the running back or the power forward on the basketball team was in my pet psychology class last semester. He's a cool guy. Not like we're best friends or anything.

The food court is awesome. That's where you guys will have lunch after the tour. I hope you kept your meal voucher. The salad bar is bigger than the one at Whole Foods out on the bypass. Smell the wood smoke? That's from the pizza oven. We're also offering vegan, kosher, and macrobiotic options. The sushi is totally fresh. All the people who work here are so great. Some of them have been here like thirty years.

That's the thing about this school. It's really unique. There's no other college like it.

SOME SCHOOLS REALLY ARE UNIQUE, of course. I was once at a dinner party with lots of high-powered people: a philosophy professor, a couple of expensive lawyers, an editor for one of the slick magazines, and a popular historian. We were talking about college, as people are forced to do when I am around.

The professor mentioned that he could often guess the kind of college a person went to from a few telltale signs.

One of the lawyers responded that whenever the subject came up in conversation, she refused, as a matter of principle, to say where she went to school.

"It's a class thing that I refuse to perpetuate," she said. "I won't ask other people that question, and I don't expect to be asked it of me either. I think it's just a subtle way of reinforcing distinctions that don't mean anything."

The editor said she agreed. "I absolutely refuse to answer," she said. "When it comes up, I just change the subject. It was a turning point in my life, it allowed me to define who I was for myself, on my own terms. But that would have happened wherever I went to school. It's just irrelevant."

"Aha," said the professor. "So you both went to Harvard."

And of course he was right. It's the most famous and most revered school in the world, and whoever enrolls in it enters a kind of freemasonry whose members always deny that the freemasonry exists. (Whoever enrolls will also graduate: Harvard doesn't permit failure among those it has chosen for itself. "If you think it's hard getting into Harvard," goes an old saying, "just try flunking out.") As higher ed has become a mass phenomenon, however, the nature of Harvard's freemasonry has changed.

"In a way you had more human diversity in the old Harvard," a friend once told me, after a lifetime of doing business with Harvard graduates. His attitude was more analytic than bitter, however.

"It used to be the only thing an incoming class shared was blue blood. But bloodlines are a pretty negligible thing. It allows for an amazing variety in human types. You had real jocks and serious dopes, a few geniuses, a few drunks, a few ne'er-do-wells, and a very high percentage of people with completely average intelligence. Harvard really did reflect the country in that way back then.

"You still have a lot of blue bloods getting in, multigeneration Harvard families. But now a majority of kids coming into Harvard all share traits that are much more important than blood, race, or class. On a deeper level, in the essentials, they're very much alike. They've all got that same need to achieve, focus, strive, succeed, compete, be the best—or at least be declared the best by someone in authority. And they've all figured out how to please important people."

Harvard grads disagree with this, of course. They like to say that the new Harvard represents the triumph of meritocracy.

No, my friend said. "It's the triumph of a certain kind of person."

I WANTED TO SEE HOW one of the world's most famous brands branded itself; the college night in the ballroom back home had offered only hints. When we arrived in Boston for our New England tour, my son insisted he had no desire to see Harvard. The next morning we made our way across the Charles River to a Harvard admissions open house.

As my wife and I hustled down Oxford Street, my son and daughter trailed even farther behind than normal.

"I'm not going to Harvard," my son said.

"So I've heard," I said.

"Me neither," my daughter said.

"Oh, come on," my wife said, momlike. "It will be fun. It's Harvard!"

The admissions office was housed in an old forbidding brick pile fronted by a stone porch and thick columns—what Tara would look like if it had been built by Calvinists. The meeting room filled quickly, and soon the crowd was lining the back wall and spilling out the doors. First we saw a video. A voice rose from the speakers: "A mosaic of faces all call Harvard home." The faces identified their hometowns, from Addis Ababa to Omaha, Baghdad to Boise, Manhattan to Moosepie, Montana. I didn't catch all the place names, obviously, but the point was emphatically made: we are ordinary folk from all over, so go ahead and apply to Harvard.

Then up popped the face of Tommy Lee Jones, a Harvard grad and just another ordinary Hollywood movie star. At Harvard his roommate was the ordinary future vice president, Al Gore.

"Some people don't apply," Jones said, "'cause they don't think they're smart enough, or wealthy enough, or have a good enough record. They're making a mistake."

A nobody kid was shown brushing his teeth in his dorm room.

"When FDR went to Harvard, he used the same sink. Whose sink will you use?"

Then came a progression of mariachi singers, hip-hop artists, army reservists, and Yo-Yo Ma, playing his cello soulfully, eyes closed. He was followed by an ordinary young man of indeterminate ethnicity who told a story with a breathlessness that suggested he didn't think anybody would believe it: he once met a professor, a Harvard professor, for coffee at a coffee shop. Then the Hollywood director Mira Nair, shown sitting in a cutting room, said: "People are born with this myth of Harvard. But I believe people should apply. You have nothing to lose and everything to gain." Next the "son of lobsterman," a horny-handed child of toil, appeared. "He didn't think he'd be accepted," Jones said. "But he applied anyway. A simple but wise, life-changing decision." No more funky fishnets for him.

An assistant admissions dean shimmered into the room as the video ended. She was accompanied by two self-possessed and well-spoken young people who described "life here at the college." The courses offered here were "amazing," they said, but they quickly assured the audience that "you're not required to take any particular course." The day of rigorous core requirements, they said, was long over.

I looked around. It was a different group of families from the others we'd been part of. More than half of them were Asian. None of the kids—not even my own—wore baseball caps or T-shirts. Many parents were taking notes. The questions they asked were brief and pointed—about the possibility of double majors, the size of premed classes, the grading schemes for various degrees. I wondered whether they were disappointed to hear the rat-a-tat answers, identical to what they had heard from other admissions deans, although offered even more mechanically. The dean said that Harvard University had more than four hundred student clubs and activities. However, if you don't find the club you're looking for, you can start it yourself and the college will subsidize it. There was even an Arnold Schwarzenegger Appreciation Society. The number of a cappella groups was thirteen.

At a question about AP classes a faint note of petulance crept into the dean's answers; she may have been upset that no one laughed at her Schwarzenegger line. How much credit will freshmen get, one parent wanted to know, for their AP classes from high school?

"None," the dean said. "Harvard does not give credit for non-Harvard courses."

What was the deadline for early decision?

"Harvard does not do early decision."

She rushed through questions about GPAs and test scores and admission rates.

"We admit roughly two thousand students," she said, and a few hundred decline the offer, but the applicant pool is so talented, "if we admitted the next two thousand students, or the *next* two thousand students, our professors would be just as happy." More than 3,300 of the 27,000 applicants scored 800 on their math SAT; another 2,500 scored the same on their verbals. Three thousand of them are valedictorians.

"But in the admissions office we're not driven by numbers or statistics or scores," she said. "Housing is guaranteed here at Harvard. The one statistic, to be honest, that drives our process more than any other is 1,652: that's the number of beds we have available for freshmen in our residence halls.

"For sure we're very interested in people of intellectual distinction," she went on. "But we admit people with weak math, weak writing scores all the time. I'd never count myself out just because of low scores. And if you don't apply you'll never know."

A man with a heavy Cantonese accent interrupted her. "How about legacies?" he asked.

"What do you mean?"

"How many of class are legacies?" he said. "Their parents went to Harvard."

"Oh, I don't have that information," she said. "I'm not sure we even keep that information."

Just a guess, then, the man persisted.

"I wouldn't want to guess."

"So you have no way of knowing?" he asked, with exaggerated incredulity. "The numbers don't exist?" His wife, short and stocky, stood next to him, staring at the dean. Their son bowed his head and closed his eyes.

"Legacy is just one of the many factors that Harvard considers," the dean said. "I like to say, 'legacy can help the wounded, but it can't raise the dead!'" She laughed uncomfortably but the father and mother still stared.

"Answer the question," another father called out.

"Maybe I can get that information for you afterward," she said, twisting one hand with the other. She moved one foot backward.

"Come on," said another parent, with just a hint of insurrection.

She was quiet a moment before surrendering. "If I had to say," she said, "thirty, maybe thirty-five percent."

There was a moment of shock before the murmuring began. The number was hard to square with the egalitarianism of the video we'd just seen. The number suggested the traditional Ivy League primogeniture.

The murmuring grew louder until another father raised a hand and the dean called on him quickly, grabbing the chance to turn the subject to Harvard's inexhaustible pool of financial aid.

We want all of you to apply, she seemed to be saying. *Of course, we won't let any of you in, but our commitment to diversity runs so deep that we want to offer as many of you as possible the opportunity to think you have a chance.*

Our guides collected us in groups and walked us into Harvard Yard—which looked . . . like Harvard Yard: the Platonic ideal of all college quadrangles, the vision that every other campus we'd seen in our travels hoped to realize. "Please look over my shoulder here to the right, please," our guide said, tossing his index finger backward. He was plump and earnest, with a slight speech impediment. "That's where Tommy Lee Jones and Al Gore roomed together, second floor. It's kind of neat: when you move in you get a list of all the people who lived in the room before you. A friend of mine got Bill Gates's room."

Our tour ended forty-five minutes later, back in the Yard, at the famous statue of John Harvard, slumped in a throne like a bored monarch. The guide pointed out the toe, where the bronze had been rubbed to a high sheen.

"It's been a tradition for a hundred years for people to rub John's left toe," he said. "We have tourists coming from all over the world to give it a rub. It's kind of funny, though. Our students have a more recent tradition. Instead of rubbing it, they pee on it."

WE DISCONTINUED OUR COLLEGE TOURS after the trip to New England. I think I was the only one who enjoyed them, and my son's preferences, once again, seemed unaffected. In the kitchens throughout the fall, with the kids back in school and the application deadlines looming, the talk among the parents often turned to campus visits, what had changed from our own time, and how much and why.

Money had most to do with it. The spectacular affluence of the last three decades showed itself in the climbing walls, in the stadiums and theaters, the pizzas pulled steaming and gooey from wood-burning ovens, and in landscaping that would wow the gardeners at Babylon. The world financial system wobbled in the summer of 2008, but the building cranes kept swinging over the campuses of American colleges and universities. Everywhere we went dump trucks and cement mixers rolled through campuses like the Third Army. The statistics at the end of that otherwise nail-biting year showed that the only sectors of the economy to thrive, to hire new workers, were health care and higher education.

Alcohol and drugs were evidently still a topic of interest on campus, to student guide and visitor alike. So was sex, as it always will be among twenty-year-olds, and among the parents of twenty-year-olds. Yet the libertinism of the seventies has been tidied up and hemmed in along with the landscaping. Sex came draped in either medicine or politics. The guides spoke often of a campus's active LGBT community, its fight for equality, and its active recruiting among "searching" and "questioning" members of the non-LGBT community. At William and Mary the student magazine *Lips: Expressions of Female Sexuality* was available for lunchtime reading at the food court. A question about sex was apt to inspire a boast about the campus health clinic and its "terrific reproductive services." We arrived at Dartmouth just in time to miss the widely advertised Second Annual Campus Sex Screening, undertaken not for titillation but for the nobler cause of clean living. "Sexperts," according to the flyers, "will be giving free demonstrations!" (Even on campus, I think it would be illegal to charge admission.) Condoms, "both glow-in-the-dark and flavored," were to be given away, along with new dental dams. The giveaway of party favors was to be followed by a "lube-tasting."

"Lots of fun!" the flyer said. "And then enjoy some Ben and Jerry's ice cream."

I'm showing my age, but back when I was a college student we didn't need free ice cream to get us to come to a sex demonstration. I suppose I can understand why the bribe is necessary. Is there a phrase in the English language less likely to arouse sexual passion than "dental dam"?

6

OBSOLESCENCE DESCENDING

Three months in twelve days—an explosive device—
Middlemarch in five hundred words—
The Books spawn a new subgenre—digging deep—
the death of Timmy—drama in real life—
a dog walker's word—Michael Phelps of the Lake—
Georgetown's epiphany

EVERY PARENT knows that life has a flawed design. I can think of several ways, both large and small, in which the whole thing is badly put together, especially when it comes to child rearing. To take a small example: through some impulse embedded in the genetic prehistory of the species, kids get fussiest just before dinnertime, exactly at the moment when you most require a little quiet and concentration to make dinner so they won't starve to death, though you might like them to. To take a large example: life ordains our early thirties, late twenties as the phase when you establish yourself professionally, which requires you to be out of the house more than you'd like; life also ordains the same period to be the prime years for having and rearing children, which requires you to be home more than you'd like. By the time things settle down professionally, and you've got more spare time to offer your children, they're out the door, and you're left to wonder what that was all about.

Design flaws just like this are everywhere built into the American system of higher learning: for some reason, life requires that the deadline for college admission essays come at the beginning of the year, guaranteeing that the final holidays at home with your high schoolers will be as horrid as possible.

For several weeks, as the deadlines approached, I had been marveling at how smoothly the application process had been going. There had been none of the Sturm und Drang, the pulling of teeth or gnashing of hair, that other parents were describing. It wasn't until Christmas was upon us that I realized why he'd been so calm about writing his essays. He hadn't been writing them.

"It won't take long," he said, after I pointed out that he hadn't much time left. He had logic on his side, as he often did—inadvertently. It wouldn't take him much time to get it done because there simply wasn't much time to get it done. QED. By mid-January, when the last of the essays was sent off and all creation seemed to relax with a sudden release of held breath, a mother told me that she and her daughter had put in three solid months of work on the essays, "every day after school and weekends."

"We did three months of work too," I said, "in twelve days."

I SAY THE *ESSAYS* WERE due, not the applications. A college application is a harmless questionnaire, easily filled out in fifteen minutes, wrapped around an explosive device, which is the personal essay. When parents talk of how harrowing the job of filing applications can be, how unfair it is that most of the applications should come due at year's end, on January 1 or 2, what they're really talking about, the true source of their bitterness, is the trauma of the essay, the thinking about and the writing of.

Essays aren't new to the process, of course. Back in the 1930s, schools typically asked for a sample of an applicant's class papers to get a sense of his writing ability. By the 1950s, most applications required a brief autobiographical statement or an explanation of why the kid had chosen one college over another. My own application statement—"Why I Want to Go to [Your School's Name Here]"—grew to the length of a paragraph before my supply of insincerity was exhausted, and none of the admissions offices bothered to press for more.

The SAT controversies have only elevated the essay's importance. In a survey a few years ago, admissions deans ranked the essay the third most important factor in their decisions, below test scores and grade-point average but far above recommendations and extracurricular activities. Practitioners of the "holistic" method say that an essay can break a tie between applicants with equivalent numbers, or lift an applicant with less impressive numbers past a higher-ranked student whose essay was deemed unappetizing.

Admissions offices are therefore ravenous for essays. If you're applying to selective schools it's rare to get away with fewer than three essays each. The Common Application—a one-size-fits-all form, available on the Web, that more and more schools have come to accept in place of their own application form—requests two essays; one is brief and informational, the second is longer and more demanding. Most schools that accept the common app add their own supplemental questionnaire requiring still more essays, in lengths ranging from 500 to 1,200 words. Five hundred words isn't much, but it can seem like *Middlemarch* if you don't have anything to say.

Which is a commoner problem than admissions people are willing to admit. As we've seen, admissions people tend to be chipper folk, serotonin-soaked and caffeinated from birth, and they assume that every high school senior should be too. In the trade, essay questions are called "prompts." It is a revealing term of art. It suggests that the purpose of the question isn't really to draw out information, it's to offer a nudge—to perch the kids at the top of a verbal toboggan run and then give a little push, so they take off yapping and don't stop till they reach the five-hundredth word. Prompts work better for some kids than others; some kids, I mean, are promptable by nature, while some could be tied to the mast and lashed with prompts till the welts rise and yet not give up a syllable. There are lots of possible reasons for their reticence. They might be stupid. They might be shy or unreflective. They might lack imagination, or perhaps they find themselves less interesting than other people, other subjects. They might for these reasons or others simply dislike talking about themselves.

In that case they're done for. Once the larger culture considered reticence a virtue; now it's cause for suspicion or evidence of derangement. It's certainly a handicap in the modern middle and high schools, where the lesson plans still bear the mark of the self-esteem movement of the 1980s and 1990s. Writing assignments are most often occasions for children to set down an inventory of their own feelings—whether they're discussing a historical event ("If you were a Cherokee, what would you say to President Jackson?"), a work of art ("Does the painting make you feel sad or happy?"), a story, a song, or something in the news. After twelve solid years of this, kids are naturally expected to require little more than a prompt to unloose a torrent of observations on the subject that has been at the very center of their schooling: the self.

The college application essay extends this practice into higher education. Surfing through college Web sites, I became a connoisseur of the prompt. "What do you think people who know you would be surprised to learn about you?" "Tell us about a moment in your life when you refused to be embarrassed." When questions refer to outside events or people other than the applicant—when they ask about a favorite teacher, a book, or a movie—they quickly get back to the main event: "How has it influenced who you are?" "Write down your thoughts and feelings about a song or book that's important to you and write a dialogue in which the work responds to you."

As the essay season approached I discovered a new subgenre of The Books, devoted exclusively to the application essay, and with time running out I left them lying casually about the house, hoping my son would pick them up out of curiosity or panic. But after several days they would be resting right where I put them. It was willful and pointed neglect. I could have strewn them like land mines on his path from bedroom to bathroom and he couldn't have avoided them more carefully. I could have wrapped them around a Baconator and he would have left them untouched.

It was probably just as well. The Books would have soured him on the task even more than he was already. I piled them up one evening with a glass of Scotch and began thumbing through. The principle of constant contradiction was much in evidence. One book insisted that anything exotic, say a foreign trip, would make the essay writer stand out from the pile; another gave a world-weary sigh and said, as Kat had advised, that admissions committees are *so sick* of foreign trips, especially those paid for by parents or sponsored as school projects. Some demanded that the essay describe an "epiphany." Others warned that an epiphany essay could be easily overdone: milk your epiphany if you must, but drop the udders before the cow moos in pain.

The authors and advice givers did seem to agree on a few things. First: the essay is the one part of the application process over which you have complete control, *so don't blow it*. Second, the essay isn't all that important, compared to grades and test scores, *so relax*.

And third: be passionate, and be passionate about yourself. "You are your best and favorite topic," as an advice book from the College Board put it. "The greatest strength you bring to this essay is seventeen years or so of familiarity with the topic: YOU. You don't have to do any research . . . you already know all you need to know . . . If you can write about wars, novels, experiments, and sonnets, writing about yourself should be simple."

This struck me as the perfect opposite of the truth. Writing about yourself may be simple; writing *well* about yourself, even if you've been hectored into it by every teacher since kindergarten, is a feat that only the most accomplished writers can pull off. Montaigne could do it, along with a few hundred of his lucky, hardworking, and gifted successors over the last four centuries. The easy way out is to settle for artifice. On the page, in the model essays The Books offered, the kids seemed to have led lives that were improbably eventful: there were heaps of spiritual awakenings, critical junctures, turning points, startling revelations, and deep-seated personal conflicts resolved with amazing speed, in just under five hundred words. They swung from wild extremes of giddy self-congratulation to near-suicidal despondency. Who knows how many of these dramatic incidents were genuine? What's certain is that the applicants were giving the admissions committees what they wanted.

In one book the admissions dean of Haverford College wrote: "The whole college application process is really a self-exploration, and the essay is a way to put your personal adventure into words. It is a summing-up, maybe a catharsis . . . You must share some part of yourself." But why? It's not as if there's no literary alternative to self-absorption. The admissions committee could ask the applicant to write an expository essay on a contemporary topic or historical incident, construct an argument, offer a brief character sketch, or describe a recent event witnessed firsthand. And these more modest prompts do pop up now and then. Until recently, for example, BSU asked students simply "to submit a piece of writing on any subject you choose, limiting your response to one page." Duke did something similar. But such questions are evidently unsatisfying, for many admissions officers see the essay as a chance not only to elicit the creativity of their applicant but to show off their own. The University of Chicago admissions committee is infamous in this regard. The questions they've written are monuments to what they must perceive as their own quirky charm:

136

Names have a mysterious reality of their own. We may
well feel an unexpected kinship with someone who
shares our name, or may feel uneasy at the thought
that our name is not as much our own as we imagined.
Most of us do not choose our names; they come to
us unbidden, sometimes with ungainly sounds and
spellings, complicated family histories, allusions to
people we never knew. Sometimes we have to make
our peace with them, sometimes we bask in our names'
associations. Ruminate on names and naming, your
name, and your name's relationship to you.

But what about the applicant who doesn't want to contemplate
his name's relationship to himself, who would find such a wallowing
in his own emotional life kind of icky? I was talking to Kat Cohen
about the application essay one day. She told me that when colleges
put her clients on a waiting list, it was often because the applicants
didn't "dig deep enough" when it came time to write their essays.

"Tell your son he has to dig deep," she said. "He has to talk
about his innermost thoughts."

I shuddered. *He's a seventeen-year-old boy!* I wanted to tell her:
Seventeen-year-old boys do not have innermost thoughts—and if
they did, neither you nor I would want to know what they are.
And in any case it's kind of impertinent of an admissions committee to make such a demand. Who are they to force a catharsis
on seventeen-year-olds? The kids are just applying to their college,
after all, not asking for their hand in marriage. This was a token
of the holistic approach: knowing what an applicant did wasn't
enough; they wanted to know who you are. It's a relatively new
idea, and very baby boomerish. The earlier notion, back before the
age of compulsive self-exposure, was that what you did was what
you were; your achievements spoke for themselves. The rest was
private life, your own business, disclosed to family and friends, if
disclosed at all.

But the questions showed even more than this. The application essay was one of those points in the process where you could see with unmistakable clarity the purpose of this new conception of college: it was supposed to be "transformational." If I had a dollar for every time I came across the word in the admissions books, I could almost afford to send my kids to college. Higher education, in this view, is not a mere contract, whereby you agree to pay a school a certain amount of money—or your parents agree to pay a certain amount of money—and in return the school agrees to give you knowledge and a degree proving that the contract has been consummated. The application essay makes it plain: they don't just want your money, they want all of you.

And if we all agree that the point of college is to remake the person instead of (merely!) to furnish the mind, then any level of nosiness and impertinence is appropriate. (Don't get me wrong: they want your money too.)

THEN CHRISTMAS WAS HERE AND he could no longer avoid the essays. I could always tell when he was working on one. He would sit at the family computer in the family room in an attitude that suggested imminent flight: perched lightly in the chair, spread-eagled, the left leg bent slightly behind, his body a quarter turn from the keyboard and computer screen. His right knee pumped like a piston. He looked as if he would bolt at the drop of a participle. Other times I caught him sitting with his head thrown back so that it dangled over the back of the chair, his eyes open but empty. Often he released a groan that rumbled up from deep in the furnace where the fires of creation raged. Or not.

"I hate writing about myself," he said through gritted teeth as I passed by one afternoon. For the common app he'd chosen to answer a question that asked him to "evaluate a significant experience, achievement, risk you have taken, or ethical dilemma you have faced and its impact on" guess who. I tossed him one of the books I'd bought, *100 Successful College Essays*. Now I was insisting.

"Maybe you'll get inspired," I said.

He cocked his head and with an uncertain look he turned the book in his hands, and I thought of the apes coming upon the obelisk in the opening scene of *2001: A Space Odyssey*. He did everything but sniff it. At length he flipped to one of the essays and read aloud: "This is the tale of being torn between two cultures . . ."

He shook his head and flipped ahead a few more pages. "I was four when my brother Timmy died . . ."

He went quiet, then almost whispered, "What am I going to write about?"

He looked at me.

"Couldn't you guys get a divorce?" he said.

"No," I said.

"It would give me something to write about. You can get back together once I'm done with the essays."

"Not going to happen."

"I wish I'd grown up in the inner city," he said.

"No, you don't."

"I wish I'd become a drug addict."

"There's still time," I said.

He lowered his forehead to the desk. "I'm a white kid living in the suburbs. I'm happy. My family is happy. My brother Timmy didn't die."

"You don't have a brother Timmy."

"Exactly. Then what am I going to write about?"

I was watching the epiphany-formation process unfold before my eyes. If you're uncomfortable writing about your inner life, and if your outer life has been happy and free of character-forming catastrophe—and remember, American society has been built precisely to allow as many people as possible to live a catastrophe-free life—then you've got one option: make it up. The artifice can take various forms. You could invent stuff from thin air. College admissions officers say this rarely happens, and that they can sniff out the concocted scenario when it does. Probably so. But there's a more common and less sinister approach. You can bend your life into a dramatic arc that it's never had, in a voice that isn't yours.

I came to think of this as the *Reader's Digest* requirement. Articles in *Reader's Digest* used to appear under various rubrics: Drama in Real Life, the Day My Life Changed, Triumph over Adversity, My Most Unforgettable Character. The incidents recounted in the articles moved along a narrative line so shapely, and so tidily resolved, as to be beyond plausibility. As *Reader's Digest* saw it, there was no problem in life that a good epiphany couldn't fix. College application essays beg for the same treatment. Our colleges and universities are asking America's teenagers to become *Reader's Digest* contributors.

After flicking through the mental index file where his most notable experiences were cataloged and summarized, my son settled finally on an incident that had taken place on a camping trip with classmates. There had been an endurance test—swimming, biking, and hiking—and he had been one of three boys who managed to swim the required distance, the rest having flopped into the lifeguard boats, sputtering lake water, defeated. I remembered vividly how proud he'd been when he came home. And with no divorces, multicultural identity crises, or sibling deaths in prospect, this sounded like the most promising topic available to him, short of outright fabrication.

After the groans and skyward glances and physical contortions, an essay finally emerged. He dropped a copy in my lap one evening after dinner. "It's not very good," he said. He wasn't being modest. The essay pulled up well short of the five-hundred-word limit. Sentences trailed off in fragments. It was wildly disorganized, everything out of place, ideas scattered here and there—a verbal version of his bedroom.

The real problem was that the essay wasn't true—wasn't true to him, I mean. He had accurately described the events, so far as I knew them. But he had related them in a voice, and with an emphasis, that weren't his. The boy in the essay struggled to finish the race; at the end he was tired but proud; he sympathized with his classmates who hadn't finished; and in his victory, accepted modestly, he learned the timeless value of persistence and determination, expressed with grim earnestness and not a trace of humor—an off-the-shelf epiphany.

I knew the truth, though, which was the masculine truth. He didn't remember the race because it proved the timeless value of persistence. He remembered the victory because it was a victory: he had competed against his classmates, friends and rivals alike, and beaten them soundly and undeniably, and earned the right to a sack dance in the end zone. He knew he couldn't say this, though, and I knew he was right. Some kinds of passion wouldn't appeal to the admissions committees. So he had resorted to another con—guessing what they wanted and then providing it in a manner that he didn't find completely false and humiliating.

"Aside from the incomplete sentences and terrible organization," I said, "it doesn't sound like you. Do you really mean all this gooey stuff?"

"Yeah," he said, looking at the computer screen. "Sure. Of course."

"I just can't hear you saying this," I said.

"That's because it's a bunch of bullcrap," he said.

I made suggestions. So did his mother. Reluctantly he went back to the keyboard to rewrite, left leg extended, torso turned, foot pumping, and thus he could be found, more often than not, for the next two days. We had begun the Great Extrusion, a painful process repeated in every household we knew of with a high school senior; parents anchoring themselves as best they could while dragging, pulling, tugging word after word and draft after draft from the insides of their mulish offspring until something presentable appeared. The Extrusion met resistance and tempers frayed. Our gentle suggestions hardened into commands, and his reluctance to rewrite curdled into outright refusal. The air in the house as Christmas came and went was charged with exasperation, defensiveness, and other anti-tidings of the season. My daughter stopped appearing in the family room for fear of the cross fire.

One night I called my friend Rob, whose son, like ours, seemed capable of producing sentences only under duress. Rob said he'd been riding his son for three solid days to finish the common app essay.

"I think I've done damage to our relationship, seriously," he said, sounding exhausted. "Maybe not permanent damage. In a few months maybe things will return to normal or something close to normal. But right now, he's so resentful, so pissed off at us—and we're pissed at him. I tried to sit next to him at the computer earlier today and he physically recoiled."

We teetered on the same precipice, my son and I, peering into the same chasm. But at last he broke. He must have realized that further resistance was futile: his mother and I weren't going away. We weren't going to lose interest. We weren't going to shut up.

There were things, however, I wouldn't say to him—things that would only be subversive. The more I thought of this essay ritual, the less sense it made. I'd interviewed a dozen admissions professionals who slagged the SAT, looked for ways to expel it from the process altogether, on the grounds that it couldn't accurately measure qualities that might make a kid a successful college student. But what qualities does the Me Essay measure? If they were trying to capture the ability to write and reason, this could be accomplished by less melodramatic means. No, the admissions essay rewarded personal qualities beyond mathematical reasoning and verbal facility. Some of the traits were appealing enough, in appropriate doses. Refreshingly effusive kids, admirably enthusiastic kids, the all-American Eddie-attaboys might very well thrive on the essay. But it would also reward other characteristics, like narcissism, exhibitionism, Uriah Heep–ish insincerity, and the unwholesome thrill that some people get from gyrating before strangers.

Which of these traits, I wondered, predicted scholarly aptitude or academic success?

I saw it at every turn, as my friend had said of Harvard: the system "privileged" a certain kind of kid. And if you weren't that kind of kid the best course was to figure out how to pretend you were.

I KNOW NOW THAT THERE was another reason for my scrupulousness—my obsessive determination that he get the essays just right. It made me feel useful. Not being the self-reflective type myself, I couldn't have admitted this at the time. Throughout the fall both my son and my daughter, only two years behind her brother, had been showing their age; I mean the independence they were growing into and were entitled to. Weekends would come and they'd be gone, off with friends for lunch, dinner, then perhaps overnight, only to resurface early Sunday evening for our traditional family pizza and homework in their bedrooms. I couldn't get used to the change, the sudden drop in the household metabolism. After seventeen years of solid activity centered on my children, I felt an unwanted obsolescence descending. I was all dressed up with nowhere to go. As always I stood ready to tell a joke, give advice, double-check homework, make lunch, offer a snack or a ride—but for whom?

How odd the college craziness is! All this expense of emotion and money and time, to make happen what I desperately didn't want to happen. But that's parenthood for you. You fulfill yourself by denying yourself, preparing the people you can't live without to live without you. The Great Extrusion was a shot at being useful in the old way. And it was annoying the hell out of him.

His essay grew duller, less plausible, with every draft. My own editing, I began to suspect, was at fault. He, for his part, had flipped strategies. From sullen and pained he had become eager to please—so eager that he had begun incorporating our suggestions indiscriminately: first from his mother, followed by my revisions of his mother's suggestions, then her reworkings of my revisions, until the essay itself broke down from multiple personality disorder.

One afternoon, after reading a fourth or fifth draft, I got jumpy. I took the dog for a walk. I ran into an acquaintance from the neighborhood doing the same. He'd graduated from an Ivy League school and now read applications as an alumni screener—flagging the most promising apps and isolating the auto-denies. As our dogs avidly sniffed each other I asked him about the essays, what he looked for.

"You just want to see a beautiful piece of writing," he said.

I was sorry I asked. Beauty: another impossible hurdle. "That's asking a lot, isn't it?" I said. I said, my kid's a smart kid, a nice kid, any school would be lucky to have him; but his aesthetic sense is not his most highly developed faculty just at the moment. Someday, sure. But now his appreciation for beauty extends to a well-timed jump shot from way downtown and ends there. It would not occur to him to attach the idea of beauty to a piece of writing.

My neighbor shrugged. "It's an exercise," he said. "You want to see if the applicant can craft something impressive."

Craft? He'd used one of my least favorite nouns-turned-into-verbs. People are "crafting" all over the place nowadays—lawyers say they craft briefs, directors craft movies, teachers craft lesson plans, and most recently I'd heard an admissions director say she "crafted" her incoming class—so I shouldn't have been surprised to see that crafting now applied to high school kids: the college applicant as artisan. When I got home, the boy was still crafting and groaning. My neighbor had convinced me that we should go literary.

As it happened, I'd written for *Reader's Digest* a few times. The editors used to love it if you began an article in medias res—in the middle of the story—to heighten drama, rather than offering events in chronological sequence. If you could begin with a bit of dialogue, even better. "Keeps the readers on their toes," an *RD* editor said to me once.

My son saw the glare of ambition shining from my face and suddenly reached for one of the advice books he'd been ignoring.

"I've got it," I said. "Let's scrap the whole thing. We'll start over in the middle—tell the story that way."

His shoulders fell. "You want a total rewrite?"

"It'll be beautiful," I said. "Instead of opening with the beginning of the race, we start telling the story near the end. And we should start with the lifeguard talking. Then we double back and tell the story from the beginning."

He looked as if I was making him swim the distance again.

"'In medias res' it's called," I said.

"In the middle of things," he said. "Latin. I've taken three years of it."

"It will keep the readers on their toes."

I'd noticed that many of the essays in the essay books used the same trick, opening in medias res, with a bracing bit of dialogue. Did too many essays begin this way? Maybe we were flirting with cliché.

The next draft was his sixth, I think. The new beginning was much better. He shrugged again when I told him this; he had ditched the eagerness strategy. I tightened up some of the phrasing, flipped a couple of sentences, cut a humorous remark that had appeared in an earlier draft. The joke seemed forced. He looked at my scratches on the page.

"That's your line that you cut, the joke," he said. "That was your idea. And the word you changed in the last line—that was yours. The whole line is yours. You're rewriting your rewriting."

Now seemed the time to try something new, to crack the ice that was forming and threatening to cut us off. I thought of dropping a draft on Kat Cohen. I knew this was her busiest time of year, however, and I didn't want to take advantage of our relationship; also, I was worried she might charge me. That left me the one alternative. Google!

When I typed in *college application essays* I got more than 64 million hits. Then I put quote marks around the phrase to narrow the search and came up with the less stratospheric but still ludicrously unmanageable figure of 65,000 hits. I scrolled and clicked through screens without end. It was like climbing a sand dune. I ignored every link to College Confidential. A high percentage of the sites advertised "editing" services that would appeal to, and squeeze money out of, anxious parents and students. For a fee you could upload a copy of your essay and have it looked at, pawed over, and otherwise rewritten by an anonymous editor working deep in the shadowy recesses of the Web. I only knew one other parent who'd tried one of these outfits. But demand must be heavy, judging by supply.

During the dot-com boom it was customary to say that the Web was the Wild West of commerce, full of prospectors, gunslingers, cardsharps, wildcatters, main chancers of every kind. Ten years on, Web commerce is more like cable TV at four in the morning, pelting the customer with promotional come-ons that even the hucksters don't expect you to believe. Operators are standing by—always, sleeplessly. You happen across some Web site and can't imagine where it originates. Who are these people? At goodessaytopics .com I read: "College application essay is perhaps the most significant and crucial type of an essay you'll ever be assigned to write, because your future depends on the results of its accomplishment. The major purpose of college application essay is to reveal your unique and genuine personality, demonstrate your writing skills, ability to organize your thoughts coherently, to build a structure of your essay logically and to express everything you think in point of the fact."

I was disheartened to think of some ESL kid Googling upon this thing and copying its broken English: "Brainstorm these ideas and add up to them those points which you are most interested in. These college application essay topics will prompt you some fresh and unconventional thoughts regarding your topic which you'll apply to your essay." At least they got the word "prompt" in there.

There were the usual medicine-show gimmicks and promotional excess, just like in three-dimensional capitalism. The bait and switch was a favorite.

"Harvard Educated Editors!" bellowed one click-through ad, and I, chumplike, clicked it. First it said that if you sent the proprietors an admissions essay it would be edited by a band of brainiacs from the banks of the Charles. I read further into the Web site and the advertised "Harvard educated editors" were demoted to the more generic "Ivy-league educated editors"—as if there weren't a big difference between the suave crew-team stylists that Harvard offers to the world and the poetry-writing ganja heads who slump out of Brown. Then on another page they had become "some of the finest editors in the world," with no mention of where they went to undergrad. The come-on had grown vague enough to be unverifiable. Who's to judge if an editor is the finest in the world? Consider, though: do the world's finest editors wind up ghostwriting college admission essays for shady Web sites patronized by nervous high schoolers whose parents have too much money? Probably not, is my guess.

The bait kept switching. I'd settled on a particular "essay editing service package"—one of the world's finest editors would edit an essay no longer than 1,200 words in forty-eight hours for only $154.99! And as soon as I selected it another screen would pop up to sweeten the offer: Buy one 1,200-word edit at the regular price of $154.99 and get a second essay edited at half the price! It was just like the Ginsu knives at four a.m. Order now and we'll send you this puppy at no extra charge. Maybe if I kept clicking *yes!* they'd send me my own Harvard English major.

I stopped at the one-essay offer: 1,200 words/48 hours/$154.99. I felt ridiculous enough already without signing on to a special deal and doubling down on my lunacy. Immediately I began to have second thoughts—wondering not whether I'd gone too far but whether I could dare go further. Using an editing service seemed ethically sound; it may be stupid but it's not immoral.

Even the College Board guidebook suggested that applicants show their essays to a teacher, parent, or friend, for suggested revisions, tightening, clarifications. But how about stupidity squared? Instead of getting an edited draft festooned with revisions from some comp-lit major, why not spend a little more and take advantage of something unambiguously unethical? Why not buy a finished essay?

I'd already come across several offers, thinly disguised, in the shadier corners of the Web. Here the commercial Internet looked less like late-night cable and more like a dark alley, with fishnetted legs in high heels stretching out of doorways and men in raincoats hunched behind Dumpsters, ready to sell you whatever you need, for a price. More than the bait and switch, the technique resembles the progressive depravity of the successful drug dealer. First the sites offer proofreading and copyediting, innocently enough; then with a few clicks they ask if you really wouldn't like a "model essay development service" instead, for just a few dollars more. "Our team," it would say, can "serve as your guides" in "crafting" the essay at every "stage of the process," from "brainstorming through finished product." A "customized sample essay" will furnish "all your college application needs." "Your personalized information" will be transformed into an "outline," which then, "with your input," becomes a "compelling, intimate narrative," thanks to "our Ivy League-trained editors." Them again.

You write the check, we write the dreck: what could be more straightforward? Yet only in a couple instances did I see the terms "ghostwriting" or "plagiarism," and never a mention of the severe consequences that might befall students who passed off the work of another as their own. Euphemisms like "essay development" avoid the issue and keep your conscience clear, and a clear conscience is expensive. The first service I found charged $1,800, which includes, first, a "personal consultation by phone with one of our Ivy League writers," and then an essay that lands, *kerplop*, in your in-box two days later, *i*'s dotted and *t*'s crossed and emotions ready for disgorging. Other services offered essays priced in the $750 range. The higher the price, the more impressive the educational credentials of the anonymous ghostwriters (from Harvard down through the lesser Ivies). I finally found a service, Doorway Learning, that modestly claimed no more than a staff of "certified writing professionals from top U.S. institutions," which could include the Mayo Clinic and Broadmoor Hospital for the Criminally Insane. At $199, Doorway was closer to my price range but still ridiculously extravagant. (My price range ranges from *inexpensive* on up to *cheap* and *not-very-much*.) I decided to pay up anyway, in the same high-spirited sense of experimentation and discovery that led me to take the SAT. Of course I had no intention of using the essay. But I was curious. And in helping my son, I still hoped to explore as many aspects of the college admissions process as I could, to gain a deeper understanding of our country, of our age, and, ultimately, of ourselves. As long as it didn't cost too much money.

BUT FIRST, AS ALWAYS, I had to fill in a questionnaire. This would familiarize the writers with my personal information, and then, in a few days, "a perfect personal statement accentuating the most important factors college admissions pay close attention to" would be delivered fully matured, like Benjamin Button. My son, of course, offered no encouragement to my little experiment. For my part, I figured Doorway's product offered the surest way to discover exactly what it was the admissions people wanted: Who would be better attuned to the tastes and crochets of admissions officers than a "certified writing professional" who spent his workday trying to please them by proxy?

My son thought I was wasting my time. His refusal to accept help from strangers draped in Internet anonymity was a matter of integrity but also of pride. (The two are often indistinguishable.) So while he worked at the family computer in the family room

I answered the questionnaire on my laptop. I worked from my memory of what he'd written about the swimming incident. There were only twenty-five questions, surprisingly. Many of them were redundant. "What about this school attracted you?" was one. The next was "What inspired you to attend this school?" "Why do you want to go to college?" and, a few questions later, "What do you expect to get out of college?" There were overlapping questions about "passions" and about "interests," about "family life" and about "home life," about "skills" and about "abilities," about "extracurricular activities" and about "things you like to do outside of school." The questionnaire itself offered an invaluable lesson for young people who would soon be called upon to fill a college blue book: say everything twice.

From the questionnaire I was sent to the payment page. I tapped in my credit-card number, recalling how, ten years ago, at the dawn of Internet shopping, I was skittish about giving my credit-card number online even to Amazon.com. Now I was happily sending it along to people who earn a living by helping kids cheat on their college applications. Progress.

We had three days to wait for our perfect essay, which would arrive on the same day that most of his applications were due. In the meantime my son now had to face the supplemental essays required by the eight schools he applied to, at least one and sometimes two per school. The swimming essay had cried uncle, having been pummeled into a form that neither pleased nor offended any of us. Now each new supplemental essay provoked its own kind of agony. "That's none of their business," I heard him hiss one evening. One of the schools had asked him to describe an episode in which he'd failed at a particular task, in the presence of other people, and to relate what the experience had taught him—about himself, natch. Breathtaking! An admissions committee that could ask such a question was either sadistic or prurient. What was this prompt supposed to prompt? There are more direct ways to humiliate a teenager, if that was the purpose.

"Up to here," my wife said, slicing her hand across her neck when I asked about her stress level. Of course, it was he, and not we, who had to sit before the screen hour by hour, wincing, clenching and unclenching his fist, lowering his forehead to the keyboard as if in a faint, pressing his brow on the keys, all so the admissions committee at Notre Dame could read in his essay that over the next four years he hoped l;akdsjfl;kjdfl;knlasdkjj;poiknn;ldskfjsljdflsdk ;jfls;dakjffjlsdjflsadjflsdfjlsdkjsldkfjlsdkjflskdfjlsweiruoaweurosudo fiu at their wonderful school.

Nothing can break the mystical connection of sympathy between parents and a child; if the kid feels a draft they catch the cold. Of course, the kid catches the cold too. My wife and I, however, had one resource that was unavailable to him: cocktail hour. The evening before we were scheduled to get our completed essay from Doorway Learning we poured ourselves stiff drinks and in the glow of the Christmas tree and flickering fire I began a philosophical conversation, provoked by the bought-and-paid-for essay that would soon arrive. Hiring a writer to write the essay and then submit it with your application was dishonest on its face, needless to say, but wasn't it really just a reductio ad absurdum, an extreme version of the game that lots and lots of families, including us, were playing already? At what point in the "editing," I wondered, does an essay cease to become the work of the applicant? When do all the changes swamp the original so that the original no longer exists? Historical collectors like to tell a story about the famous ax once owned by Abraham Lincoln. It sold for millions of dollars, even though since Lincoln's time the head had been replaced three times and the handle twice.

From what I could tell, a similar process was at work all over America as college deadlines bore down. In our case, all those inserted sentences, substituted paragraphs, potted insights, word changes, and shifts in tone that his mother and I had suggested, and that he, to shut us up, had accepted, must have by now formed the bulk of at least a few of his essays. When I floated the question to our friends, it seemed to make them uncomfortable—with the exception of my friend Rob. "I let him have a few of his crappy sentences, sure," Rob said. "That way it still looks like he wrote it. And he's got some sense that it's still his own work. But my God, I couldn't let him turn in some of this stuff. For one thing, it made no sense." The future of our children is too important to be left to our children.

"Oh, please," my wife said, when I raised the point. Though she is part German and part French, she is impatient with philosophical reflection. This was doubly true when it came to getting our son into college. She knows most of the same professional writers I do, and among them are a few well-paid scribblers whose work seldom appears in print until it has been patted, plumped, stretched, and kneaded, and—to say it plainly—rewritten by protective editors, who remain anonymous while the writer accepts the money and the praise, usually without much humility. She mentioned them now. "How come xx and yy get to take credit for their articles? I'll tell you why: because the articles are still theirs. Right?"

"Technically."

"Right. Then these application essays are still his."

Short of outright fraud, we were going to tolerate whatever helped his chances to get into BSU. Including BS.

The Doorway essay materialized in my e-mail queue the next day. It was, as movie critics always say about Meryl Streep's acting, a revelation. On two sheets of paper the anonymous writer had managed to include every annoying tic and affectation I had come to loathe in the essay books. I don't know what I was expecting, but all I could think was: So this really is what the admissions people want. Each detail was intensified into vivid implausibility. The swim across the lake was now extended into a swim around the perimeter of the lake; his achievement in managing not to drown was Michael Phelps–like. In the questionnaire I had mentioned a story about my son's mowing the yard of a widowed neighbor. In the hands of the hired hand this had ballooned into an example of "my community service": he had been "serving my community" by "helping elderly citizens manage their yard work and other domestic chores." It sounded like he'd started the Salvation Army Gardening Corps.

The essay was an aerial view of a boy's life: the teen years as seen from ten thousand feet, through a cloud of wishful thinking. Even in exaggerated form the details were lost in the sweep of generalization. Sometimes a detail is just a detail, but here each detail, when it was glimpsed through the cottony prose, became a symbol of something grand and far beyond itself. The swim strokes were the independent spirit challenging the current of convention and conformity. "With each passing challenge in life, I grew more resilient." Then the strokes became a symbol of his studiousness: "One stroke at a time, I am prepared to study diligently and become a valued contributor in this learning environment, one step at a time." Step, stroke—what's a little mixed metaphor when such grand themes are in play? Then again, maybe he meant to imply the boy could walk on water.

It would be a miracle, yes, but perfectly in character. This was one fine applicant, if he did say so himself! The essay was an explosion of self-flattery—just like the essays in the essay books. Every sentence contained a little stink bomb of braggadocio. "With my personal attributes of strength, determination and perseverance . . . I also possess a set of positive values, virtues and character traits . . . I'm physically and mentally grounded . . . my personal attributes of strength and perseverance . . . I bring with me a sense of respect . . . my strong collaboration and teamwork skills . . ."

If I were an admissions dean and an applicant sent me an essay that strutted like this one, I'm not sure if I'd accept him or spank him. But there was no question our hired hand thought he knew the magic words, or word, that would make an admissions committee coo: "I would be proud to work collaboratively with diverse populations to solve problems . . . I seek to join the diverse population of students . . . my readiness for greater challenges in the diverse learning environment . . . my enthusiasm for history, diplomacy and cultural diversity . . ." Every fiftieth word in the essay was "diversity." I counted.

The e-mail came with a cover note in which once again there was no mention of plagiarism and its dangers, either practical or moral, and by the look of it this essay was meant to be camera-ready, waiting to be bundled up and beribboned and sent off to the lucky schools. I tried to convince myself that my little investigation was worth the two hundred bucks. The essay I'd bought wasn't much different from the examples in The Books, and certainly it was no worse. It confirmed my view of the essay culture; with the exaggerated expectations, the demand for "passion," and the intrusive questions, the admissions process had already managed to turn essay writing into a scam, and hiring somebody to write one was just a way of scamming a scam. It also cast a new light on the essays my son had been laboring over and that I and his mother were primping: they were better than this thing. Reading the paid-for essay, I felt the anxiety unexpectedly begin to lift.

I showed it to him and he read it quickly and set it aside with a shrug. He had another essay for me to read. He had found a question he liked, from a school that didn't ask him to wade into the slough of the self and fish out another moment of rapture, mortification, or enlightenment that would make him a stronger, more open, and more diverse individual committed to applying his widely recognized skills of tolerance and hard work at the awesomely beautiful campus of . . .

The good question came from Georgetown University—a place he had considered a reach school, a fond but faraway dream, until his ardor to go there was inflamed by the reasonableness of its application. It asked applicants to write about a current world crisis (so many to choose from) and to propose some course of action. He treated the opportunity as a liberation and threw himself into the job. He chose to write about the sudden outbreak of piracy in the Gulf of Aden, an issue then much in the news. He researched the pirates, documented their villainy, plumbed their tactics, and in a day or two had developed a three-point plan for running the buggers out. These he presented with the cocksureness of an editorial writer for *The Economist,* the kind who always says: "The crisis will only be averted if the world community undertakes the following three actions immediately."

"That's really good," I said, and meant it. The prose was clear, the argument tight, the evidence ample, and the sentences marched one after another in a logical sequence toward a reasonable conclusion. These five hundred words told more about what kind of student he'd be than all the epiphanies, embarrassments, and emotional breakthroughs put together.

"It's like a vacation," he said, "not having to answer another one of those stupid questions."

I'M NOT SURE, AND I'M not going to ask him, but I think the Georgetown vacation proved a kind of turning point. With two days to go he still faced a handful of essays, and the prompts were still silly when they weren't obnoxious or pointless—"Tell us in an essay what essay question you think we should ask"—but he answered them on his own terms, evidently less worried about what we or the admissions committee would say. Craving a tidy narrative arc myself, I'd like to think this was the result of his own epiphany, but more likely he was suddenly at ease because there wasn't time to waste on the alternative. Whatever the explanation, his remaining essays were often funny, like him. The themes were sharper, and there were fewer fancy words. They weren't written the way I'd have written them, but it was too late for much parental editing, and besides, I finally remembered, these were his essays not mine. Something genuine crept in, the tension drained away as a knotted-up muscle loosens under applied pressure. I didn't want to admit it, but there was maybe something in what Kat had told me the winter before, echoed in a few of The Books. The admissions ordeal was beginning to look—I winced again at the phrase—like a process of personal growth.

There was a final frenzy the night of January 1, when half a dozen apps were due at once. All the applications were in digital form, of course. We sat at the computer together in the darkened house, going over the forms screen by screen, tracing our fingers down line by line, scanning for typos, double-checking punctuation, making sure the essays had uploaded properly, all as the chimes of midnight approached. He clicked the last submit button with fifteen minutes to spare.

He slept late the next morning. I felt as if we'd been through a battle together. I got up early, leaving my wife asleep in bed. I crept to the next room and called up my e-mail. Sometime after midnight I'd gotten a bulletin from College Parents of America, a mailing list I'd joined the year before.

"If you thought applying to college was stressful," it read, "applying for financial aid is even more daunting."

7

THE UNANSWERED QUESTION

Patton on the radio—meeting the EFC—
bird sanctuaries and tuition bills—
the Expecter in his lair—fogs and fevers and FAFSA—
another race against time—
introducing Professor Vedder—
tuition discounting, ours and theirs—
what if the bubble bursts?

I WAS driving to work: a Saturday morning, the plucky sunshine of late winter, an open freeway into town, no traffic, foot heavy on the pedal, my hatchback econobox wheezing to life and pushing sixty. I switched on the radio and got a talk show.

"For the past year I've been studying this," said a voice. "I mean, really studying. You have got to do your research. You have got to do your homework. Make sure you know precisely what's available . . . and then—then—you formulate your strategy."

It was a minute before I realized he was talking about my obsession, and another minute before I realized that once again I was hearing a person who had obsessed about my obsession much more productively than I had.

"I look on this as a partnership with my daughter," the voice said. The words came quickly. "It's been a life experience, and let me tell you, we've had a great time. We picked our schools, we categorized them, we laid out a strategy for each one. We knew strengths, weaknesses, good departments, bad departments. A ball. It's been a ball."

A caller came on. He asked the voice what his "strategy" was.

"It changes school to school, of course," the voice said, all business. "You don't have one of these one-size-fits-all strategies. One size does not fit all."

He sounded like General Patton. He was kicking some candy-butt.

"The strategy right now, at this stage, is all about fiscal issues. FAFSA. Get to know that term. Free Application for Federal Student Aid. This is what will determine how much this whole thing is actually going to cost you. When should you get started on FAFSA? Now. Yesterday. Last month. It's very difficult, very complicated. Get your EFC and then go look at those loans. Look at all the aid that's out there. Get yourself in the position to maximize that potential."

He went on for a long time, breathlessly, until the break. Now that the apps were sent off, I had started to feel that the process was somehow under control. But suddenly I felt the way I'd felt when I first read Kat Cohen's book on the train to New York, utterly absorbed, slightly clammy, within shouting distance of a mild panic. FAFSA? EFC? WTF? Somebody honked. I looked at the speedometer. On the open highway I'd slowed the econobox to twenty miles an hour.

THE COST OF COLLEGE IS the consuming preoccupation for parents, of course, and a major source of the craziness. It's not hard to see why. I graduated from a small liberal arts college in 1978. My annual tuition bill was $5,100. If my school's tuition had tracked inflation, the bill today would be $16,500. Instead it's nearly

$40,000—an exponential rise repeated at nearly every school in the country.

But unlike other questions related to college admissions—how do I make my kid write the essay, do we really have to do a tour, who designs these stupid applications, when will it all be over?—how to pay for school is a peculiarly sensitive matter. With the Kitchen People I could start a good thirty- or forty-minute chain rant by asking about the college counselors at their kids' high schools. But when I'd ask about college costs I'd provoke a quick Vesuvius-like burst, followed by a slow glide into silence, a lot of foot-shuffling and ceiling glancing, until people drained their cups and wandered off for a refill. Nobody likes to talk about money, especially when you're being reminded you don't have enough of it.

What might be delicate or unseemly in normal life, however, is daily meat for the butt-wiggling exhibitionists on the Internet; otherwise there would be no blogs. No allowance is made for financial reticence. "How to Pay for College" is a favorite cybersubject, and the resources at first glance look inexhaustible. But when it came to finance I restricted myself for the most part to College Board and the Department of Education Web sites. I took their directives to be authoritative. (If you can't trust an agency of the federal government, who can you trust?) By the time I was through collecting material about college costs, I had enough documents to make several impressive new stacks in the dining room. There were booklets, worksheets, request forms, disclaimers, power points, suggested guidelines, official guidelines, disclosures, charts, backgrounders, tables, monthly planners, and FAQs beyond number. Usually the sheets showed ranked masses of bullet points with impenetrable headings: "ICR Consent to Disclosure of Tax Information," "Repayment Plan Selection," "DCL GEN-04-04 General Guidance for FRAC Participants," "Fafsa4caster," "Income Based Repayment Selector," and "FFEL Convertible-rate Interest Rates Calculation Sheet." I could concentrate on them for no longer than forty-five seconds at a time. Then I'd look up and hear Patton: "Very difficult, very complicated."

Among those reams of paper many pages were pure salesmanship—and what the CB and the Education Department were selling was, once again, college itself, the raw idea of it, quite apart from any considerations that might draw a kid to one particular school or another, or, heaven forbid, toward a future of work and family without higher ed. The message was unmistakable: When it comes to college, you should just go. Don't worry so much about the money. You can handle the money. Go. The money—we'll help with the money. Just go. *Go,* for crying out loud.

One of the first sheets I acquired from the CB, under the section College Costs, set the tone. It offered a little *USA Today*–like charticle—half chart, half article—headlined "Keep Rising Prices in Perspective."

"Media reports," the sheet said, "can be intimidating. Don't let the sticker prices scare you." Damn lyin' media.

"There's no escaping the fact that college costs are rising," the sheet acknowledged, though I knew that if there were a way of escaping the fact, the College Board would have found it.

"But there is good news," it continued. "There is more than $143 billion in financial aid available." (That number—$143 billion, the pot of gold—was repeated frequently, endlessly, in the documents.) The chart that followed showed two columns. On the left was the bad news. On the right was the good news, offered as refutation of the bad, in a box labeled "But did you know that . . ."

So in the left-hand column we saw that last year tuition rose by 5.9 percent at private schools and 6.4 percent at public schools. "But did you know that . . ." gave the rebuttal in the right-hand column: "About 56 percent of students enrolled at four-year colleges attend institutions that charge tuition and fees of less than $9,000 per year." Good for them. And the other 44 percent?

On the left, the bad news: "The average surcharge for out-of-state students at public institutions is $10,867."

Then the good: "But did you know that . . . About two-thirds of all full-time undergraduate students receive grant aid."

On the left: "Students will pay on average from $381 to $408 more than last year on room and board."

"But did you know that . . . More than $143 billion in financial aid is available to students and their families."

Actually, we did know that, since it had already been printed right there at the top of the page. The rebuttals weren't very effective, if you thought things through. It was small comfort to know that this problem of rising costs was solvable, but only so long as the family agreed to go deeper in debt or accept repeated handouts. Maybe it's good news that $143 billion was available for aid. But isn't it bad news that we need the $143 billion in the first place?

"Consider college an investment," the information sheet concluded, its manner calm and reassuring. Then this College Board charticle quoted a study from the College Board that said people who earned a degree from a college, schools such as those that make up the College Board, earn 60 percent more than workers with only a high school degree—adding up to $800,000 over a lifetime.

"Whatever sacrifices you and your child make for his or her college education in the short term are more than repaid in the long term."

I'd noticed something interesting about these communications from the higher-ed establishment. The only time they spoke of higher education in business terms, weighing costs and benefits, was in the middle of a come-on to parents and students, most of whom were presumably comfortable with seeing life in terms of commercial transactions. Otherwise the literature treated higher ed as a spiritual realm, filled with mystery and magic, immune from the worldly pressures of costs and benefits.

The cultlike disingenuousness of it was galling. Much of the stuff I'd accumulated from the College Board was thinly disguised propaganda of this kind—prettied up in numbers, but just as self-serving as anything you'd expect from a business lobby.

"Don't let the sticker price scare you," the next sheet said, ramming the message home. "Financial aid often makes up the difference between what you can afford to pay and what college costs." And just so you don't forget: "Education loans are also an appropriate way for families to pay for college."

At every turn, an unwary parent or student would find information shaded in this way, always to the advantage of the institutions that furnished the information. This was another scheme I'd seen in Washington politics, over and over. I'd learned not to trust "scientific studies" about carbon emissions written by think tanks subsidized by oil companies. But when it came to American higher education, especially the glories of subsidy and debt, we were expected to rely on the touts of colleges, the College Board, and the Education Department, the whole higher-ed establishment.

The favored technique was misdirection. Oil companies perfected it in the field of public relations. They'd air TV commercials showing endangered cormorants and egrets gliding gracefully over swamp grass, as though the companies were in business for the sole purpose of creating bird sanctuaries—and never mind the spill gurgling and spreading just out of camera range. In the same way colleges are happy to boast of the munificent sums of financial aid available to pay a family's enormous tuition bills. But please don't ask why the bills are so enormous in the first place.

SO IT WAS GALLING, DISINGENUOUS. Cynical misdirection. Fine. Like every other nonrich family, we still had no choice but to press ahead in a search for ways to pay. Of the schools my son applied to, only the in-state schools, BSU and Tech, would cost us $20,000 a year or less for tuition, fees, and room and board. The other schools on his list cost much more. Three of them charged more than $50,000 a year: Georgetown, Notre Dame, and Vanderbilt. UNC at Chapel

Hill was slightly more affordable at $36,000. And over the next four years we could expect the prices to rise at a rate far beyond normal inflation. A tuition bill we could almost afford this year might be out of reach by the time he was a senior.

But the question of what we could afford was not a question that we were going to decide for ourselves. That is a calculation for the government to make. This is when I was introduced to the EFC, the "expected family contribution" that the radio Patton had mentioned. EFC is the most mysterious magical formula since the death of Morgan le Fay. As colleges never fail to point out, a large majority of students get some kind of cut-rate loan, grant, or scholarship, either from the government, a bank, or the school itself, to help them meet costs. EFC is designed by the government to assess a family's income and savings and then, in the government's phrase, determine "the amount a family can be expected to contribute to a student's college costs." The difference, presumably, will be met by subsidies, loans, and gifts.

Note the passive voice. *Can be expected:* Who does the expecting? And how does the expecter calculate how much he will expect me to pay? A reasonable assumption is that somewhere in the basement of the Department of Education sits a moist, heavyset, bespectacled fellow with an overstuffed pocket protector splitting the seams of his shirtfront, hunched in a windowless cell lit only by a computer screen that glows with algorithms of his own devising. He's the Expecter: unseen, unfathomable, and unspeakably powerful, like Blofeld in the James Bond movies, without the expensive cat. Or the lap. The most powerful people in government are always anonymous.

I went through my reams to understand how the Expecter works, dusting for his fingerprints. The actual mathematical formula by which this calculation is made—by which the federal government informs you how much of your kid's tuition you can afford to pay—is devised by the staff of congressional committees and implemented by the Education Department's Expecter. But its details are buried under layers of percentages, ratios, and fractions. I found hints of it at last on one of the worksheets I had collected.

There are more than a hundred line items in the FAFSA—the actual application for aid. Only a handful of the line items determines your EFC. Total income, for example: to calculate your income, the Expecter allows you to deduct your income tax and part of your Social Security tax from your wages. The Expecter also bestows an "income protection allowance"—a portion of your income that he will not require you to pay out for college tuition. His "asset protection allowance" allows you to keep some portion of your assets—savings, checking account, investments, if any—so you don't have to pay them in tuition; the precise dollar figure is revealed in a cluttered and complicated chart. Together these two allowances constitute all of the worldly goods that you are allowed to keep when your kid goes off to school.

Still the Expecter is not done. He makes more adjustments to your income and assets. For no discernible reason, for example, some of the income figures are divided by .12, and then, further along in the formula, by .20. Another "protection allowance" appears, for $3,080, and then another assessment of .50 is made, and another of .22. It makes no more sense doing it than reading about it. Why .12, why .20? Why not .13 and .18? Why $3,080 rather than a good, clean $3,000? Only the Expecter knows.

THERE IS ONE PARTICULARLY GENEROUS aspect to FAFSA. And I, along with parents everywhere, would be grateful for it, if it were real. FAFSA guidelines said the form wasn't due until the end of June. The late deadline imparted a welcome and mistaken sense of composure. By June we would know which schools, if any, had accepted my son's application, and we would have a firm handle on how much it was going to cost. Our tax forms would be safely filed, so we would have accurate figures about income and savings, and the computations could be done at leisure, almost. Indeed, if the financial aid process began and ended with FAFSA, it might be manageable.

But the reprieve was an illusion. In addition to FAFSA, most colleges require that even more elaborate aid applications be filed with the College Board. The CB's iDoc service was to collect copies of the family's tax returns so they could be cross-checked with FAFSA. The College Board also required the CSS Profile, asking all the questions that are on FAFSA and giving us the opportunity to answer them twice, plus other, equally intrusive questions the College Board has thought up on its own. These documents are due at the beginning of March. And since the College Board applications can't really be completed until the FAFSA is completed, the effective deadline for anyone seeking student aid is March 1—before taxes are due, and two months after the college apps are due, and, for most students, several weeks before they receive acceptances or rejections from their schools.

After dinner on February 28, with twenty-four hours to spare, I was at our basement computer, logging on to the Web to find the FAFSA. The guidelines told me what documents to have at hand. I hadn't done my most recent tax return yet—April 15 was six weeks away—so I had to rely on last year's return to estimate income figures. I had our checkbook next to the keyboard, and the statements from our savings account and our 401(k), and the mortgage statement too: my life in numerals. Some of The Books say that parents should make their kids fill out the FAFSA and the other financial aid documents that the College Board demands. The idea was horrifying. It suggested an unseemly commingling of roles that had been carefully defined and separated for as long as my son and daughter had been alive: household finances were a concern of parents, frittering them away was the job of children. I'd sooner have them rifle my high school diary or interview my college girlfriends than nose through my bankbook. I'd yell at them in either case.

I typed *www.fafsa.com,* which unexpectedly led me to a "student financial aid advisory service," a private business charging

165

$99.99 to help me fill out my FAFSA form. Instead of the orgasmically happy kids that were featured on other college Web sites, it had pictures of middle-aged parents looking worried, far past the point where orgasms were even a theoretical possibility.

I tried Fafsa.gov, which took me to the Department of Education Web site. When I tried to access the form a box popped up to tell me the departmental site couldn't accept my Web browser.

To make my FAFSA preparation as smooth as possible, I had stupidly installed the latest version of the browser that afternoon. The FAFSA site would only accept the earlier version. I didn't know how to uninstall my browser and reinstall the earlier version, so I packed up my documents, climbed the stairs, and sat down at our second family computer.

That computer used the earlier browser. It was four years old and sclerotic with unwanted malware and ancient viruses. I unpacked my documents again, called up the form, and waited for it to load. I made excellent time filling every single blank on the first two screens. Then, with a single stroke, I deleted all my entries. I started over.

THE GOVERNMENT SAYS IT SHOULD take an hour to fill out the form. It was midnight when I finished the FAFSA, two a.m. when I filed my College Board profile and the iDoc. I slept a fitful sleep and went to lunch with Rob the next day, seeking sympathy and fellowship. I knew he'd spent the previous evening doing the same thing. He looked rattled. Worse: he looked like I looked.

He told me he'd just read a story about FAFSA in the *New York Times*. It said some people were paying as much as $1,500 to hire people to fill out the form.

"Worth every penny," he said. "If I could afford it. But then if I was the kind of guy who could afford to spend fifteen hundred on something like the FAFSA, I wouldn't be the kind of guy who needed to fill out a FAFSA."

He put his palm to his forehead. "You're supposed to pay for the CSS Profile, aren't you?" he said. "On that last screen?"

"Yes," I said. The College Board charged a nine-dollar processing fee, and then twenty-five dollars to give a single school access to your financial profile, and sixteen dollars for every school after that. I'd put more than a hundred dollars on my MasterCard.

"I woke up at four in the morning in a sweat, certain I forgot to pay," he said. "I'm pretty sure I didn't pay. I was in such a fog."

I hadn't been in a fog. It was more like a scalding fever. The adjective I'd heard most often to describe the student aid forms was "proctological." But the intrusiveness was just for starters. The duplication of the questions, the crankiness of the software, the clutter and confusion of the forms themselves . . . in the dead of night, before my wheezing computer, I had got annoyed, then angry, then righteously pissed. At the end of the iDoc interrogation, after you've exposed the entrails of your pitiful finances, sent them over the Internet to be picked through and laughed at by who knows what computer hacker in Mumbai or Nova Scotia, fished your credit card from your wallet, and clicked through to what you think is the last screen that will show your bill so you can pay the inflated fees, what should pop up on your computer monitor but a special notice from the College Board . . . "A Special Offer! 30% off Retail Price! A new book!" Published by the College Board, of course. *Meeting College Costs:* "This indispensable resource . . . Learn about alternatives . . . Get answers to common questions . . . $14.95!"

This last bit of hucksterism had sent me around the bend, but I didn't have far to go. It was late, my family had long since gone to bed, my head clanged like a dinner bell, I was tired and full of self-pity. I was sick of the College Board, the schools, the nickel-and-dime expenses, the vast, unblinking federal government, the imperturbable bureaucrats and their impenetrable forms. I'd had enough of the Expecter, whoever he was, and the entire process of financial aid—and when I paused to reflect on why I was angry, I came up with the answer: *Because they've made it inconvenient for me to get free money.*

My fever broke right about then. So this is what it did to you! Here it was firsthand, in miniature: the psychological cost of beggardom, assuming the role of supplicant, applying to be a ward of other people's generosity. I hadn't gotten any money yet and already my demands were escalating. Not only should the money be free, and come in large sums, and be spent only on my son; it should also be effortless. I'm not sure what I expected: maybe that I'd make a phone call to the Department of Education and they'd just hand it over, direct-deposit a handsome chit in my checking account, slip it into a money-market fund supervised by my own personal government-appointed financial adviser.

But shouldn't it be kind of difficult to get free money? I could see how easy it was as a supplicant to descend into pure appetite: demanding more convenience, more solicitude, more easy access, more, more, more money.

If the "financial aid process" was supposed to be like the admissions process—one more adventure in personal growth—then I was failing utterly. I wasn't growing, I was shrinking, getting smaller by the minute.

I mentioned this to Rob at lunch. "I felt like a jerk," I said. "It's kind of a reprehensible attitude, really, like a reverse JFK. 'What's my country going to do for me?'"

"What's the alternative?" he said. "You're going to need that money. I'm going to need that money. What happens if your kid doesn't get into BSU? What if you're paying fifty grand for Notre Dame instead of twenty for BSU? Where's the money come from?"

I ran through the available options, as if he didn't know them himself. I pointed out that there were private loans at exorbitant rates, more loans at subsidized rates, a second mortgage on the house, a second job for either me or my wife or both, or, failing that, selling narcotics and, if necessary, my body.

Rob didn't give a hint of a smile. He was staring at his bialy. "Why the hell does it cost so much anyway?"

IT WAS A QUESTION WE'D asked each other a dozen times, and neither of us had found a satisfactory answer. Then I heard about Richard Vedder, distinguished professor of economics at Ohio University, who's studied college tuition so long, so thoroughly, and so honestly that college administrators can't stand him.

I made an appointment to see him at an office he uses part-time in Washington. That morning the *Chronicle of Higher Education* ran an article about the steady increase in college costs; most mornings the *Chronicle* runs an article about the steady increase in college costs. "For the nation's elite private colleges," the article began, "$50,000 is fast becoming the new normal." At least fifty-eight schools were now charging more than the magic fifty for tuition, fees, room and board. The year before, in 2008–2009, only five schools had cost more than fifty thousand a year. And six years ago, when my son was in middle school, only two schools cost more than *forty* thousand a year; now 224 colleges and universities charged more than that.

In a hundred different ways my heart was breaking at the thought of my son leaving home, and yet . . . at this rate, if I didn't shove him out the door soon I was going to be looking at sixty, seventy thousand dollars a year. And my daughter wasn't far behind. I hated to see the kids go, really, but now it was a race against time.

Richard Vedder once did a calculation along similar lines, using his alma mater as a test case. He matriculated at Northwestern University in 1958, when the annual tuition was $795. That sum represented about 15 percent of the annual median family income at the time. By 2003, forty-five years later, annual tuition was $28,000, or 53 percent of median family income. If the rate of increase in tuition and family income holds steady, by 2048, Northwestern's tuition will be priced at nearly double the median family income—

meaning that the average family would have to work two years to pay one year of tuition at a selective university.

Vedder is always tossing out calculations like this, finding new ways to make plain what parents know in their bones and feel in their bank accounts, the mind-boggling, impoverishing rise in the price of going to college. One historical study shows that college tuition, adjusted for inflation, increased between 2 and 3 percent a year from the beginning of the last century till the mid-1970s. Back then, the old wheeze among college presidents was that a year of college shouldn't cost more than the price of a midsize Chevrolet. Around 1975, however, something happened. College costs detached themselves from the rest of the economy and, like a dirigible unloosed from its mooring, angled sharply skyward. Annual increases of 5 and 6 percent above inflation have been common ever since. In one year alone, 2003, average tuition rose 14 percent. The annual cost of a typical private college went—studies show—from $3,663 in 1975 to $34,132 in 2009, nearly a tenfold increase. Add in another eight or ten thousand for room and board, and a parent could buy a couple Chevys with what he was paying for college, with enough left over for a Harley.

Through boom years or bust, it doesn't matter, health care and higher ed are the two growth sectors of the American economy, in size and cost. In the meantime, though, health care has made great advances in quality—in technology, in drugs, in types of care. No one could claim similar improvements in the quality of higher education. The campuses are very nice, as we saw on our college tours, the landscapes exquisite, the food courts dazzling, the climbing walls sturdy and challenging. But improvements to the physical plant alone can't account for the huge increases: the price of construction and food service in the general economy hasn't risen as fast as the cost of college room and board. So why does it cost so much?

It's odd: the question of rising health-care costs has generated a vast industry of econometricians and other number jockeys who make a living studying its causes and effects—the experts get hired by every interested party, from hospitals to insurance companies, from nurses' unions to Congress itself. By comparison the same question about college has gone relatively unexamined. It's a rock that experts seem reluctant to kick over, probably because so many of the experts are protected by the rock, clinging to tenure. Vedder is the most prominent exception. So when I went to see him, I asked him the unavoidable question that never gets answered.

"YOU WANT MY SHORT ANSWER?" he said. "This is my simple, one-sentence answer to why colleges keep raising their tuition: because they can!" He let out a short laugh, a high and wild sound. "I mean, who's going to stop them? Parents? The government? There's nothing stopping them—literally nothing."

He gripped the sides of his chair and half lifted himself in the air—a theatrical gesture that I came to expect when some point of intellectual contention roused him, which was often. He was dressed in a short-sleeved white dress shirt stretched a bit too tight across his frame, with a tie knotted indifferently a quarter inch below his collar button. His hair was thinning and scattered across his forehead like loose straw. His reading glasses were in constant motion, falling from the top of his head to the tip of his nose as he leaned back and grabbed his wrists behind his head, pulling figures and anecdotes out of the air. He once called himself "the original absentminded professor," and he looks every inch the part. We were sitting with Dan, one of the graduate students who trails in his wake to ensure he has whatever papers he needs and is headed in the right direction. "Sometimes," he told me, "I need help getting from Point A to Point B."

"Think of the question in terms of incentives," he said. "There's no incentive to save money and keep costs down. All the incentives run the other way. Look at the way a school operates. They call it 'shared governance.' What that means is, everyone thinks they run the place. The trustees think they run it, the alumni think they run it, the state legislature thinks they run it, if it's a public university. At some schools they have student trustees and various boards filled with students—and they think *they* run it.

"And then there's the poor president. His job actually *is* to run it. To do this he has to buy off all these various groups and make them reasonably happy. You buy off the alums by having a good football team. A good football team costs money. You buy off the faculty by giving them good salaries. You let them teach whatever they want, keep their course loads low. You buy off the students by not making them work too hard. I'm serious about that: there's grade inflation, there's not too much course work, the reading assignments given to students are much less than they were forty years ago. You make sure the food is good and the facilities are nice. And you buy off the legislators and trustees in various ways: tickets to the big football games, admit their kids if they apply, get a good ranking from *U.S. News.* All this costs huge amounts of money. No wonder universities are expensive!"

And no wonder they don't much like Professor Vedder. Among the higher-education establishment Vedder's work is no more popular than Bob Morse's rankings, and for similar reasons. ("I still occasionally get invited to establishment conferences," he said. "I think they just want to get a look at this curiosity, this strange creature.") Like Bob, Vedder declines to see college as a romantic endeavor that should be insulated from the market pressures that most of us are subject to. Higher education, for him, is a subject as suited to cold-eyed analysis and dispassionate judgment as any other. Among the professors of economics and education who have studied the rising costs of college—studies that generate amazing amounts of statistics, as you'll soon see!—only Vedder has consistently drawn a conclusion that is less than flattering to the institutions that pay the salaries of professors of economics and education.

Why are there no incentives to cut costs? It's the same problem that afflicts health care: a large portion of the people consuming the services aren't paying for the services out of their own pocket. The costs are picked up by third parties. In health care, that includes the government and employers paying insurance premiums. In the case of higher ed it's the government again, plus subsidized loans and scholarships that pass through the schools themselves. The self-regulating system of supply and demand breaks down.

Normally, an increase in price reduces demand, which in turn moderates prices. In higher ed, that doesn't happen. When the prices rise, subsidies increase. With more Pell grants available for low-income students, more scholarships and cheap loans given to the better-off families, the schools are free to raise tuition again. This vicious cycle was demonstrated a few years ago by two brave economists from the University of Oregon. They amassed an immense database about schools over a ten-year period. They found that "each increase in Pell aid is matched nearly one for one by tuition increases" at private schools. A similar link exists between increases in aid and increases in out-of-state tuition at state universities.

Just because you get more aid, in other words, doesn't mean you'll get more buying power in the college marketplace: the extra dollars will likely be swallowed up in tuition hikes. This is one reason why increases in Pell grants haven't led to an increase in the number of low-income students attending college, the same students whom the grants were meant to help. Disadvantaged students make up roughly the same proportion of college-going students as in 1970, when the huge increase in federal aid began—right before the explosion in tuition prices.

But the market isn't just distorted for low-income students. Normally, the market "punishes" decisions that are financially irrational. In higher ed, you can be as irrational as you want. With aid money and subsidized loans sloshing around, the penalty for making an irrational decision is vastly reduced—*after all, it's not my money*—and therefore middle-class consumers are, no surprise, more likely to make crazy decisions. And let's face it: sending your kid to a selective school that you can't afford, especially when a good education is easily obtainable at a less expensive school elsewhere, is crazy. But! If you're getting a discount on the price, through loans or grants, the decision, at first glance, looks less crazy.

Our family was an instant case. My wife and I couldn't afford to send our son to Georgetown, by any rational measure. But that wasn't going to stop me, if he got in. I was going to borrow against savings or the value of my house, or, if we got lucky, I'd hold out my hat to catch a grant or a subsidized loan tossed down by the gods of financial aid. There are thousands of panting parents just like us. What reason would Georgetown have to lower its price? And Georgetown knows, moreover, that it will pay no penalty in lost customers if it jacks up the price next year, and the year after that—so long as the aid increases too.

THE SURREAL METHOD OF FINANCING that makes this possible is called tuition discounting. On examination it offers few benefits to the customer, and I can't imagine it surviving in any part of the economy where normal rules of competition apply. One group must find it congenial, however. Tuition discounting greatly enlarges the power of college administrators, the admissions committees in particular—and especially the "enrollment managers," admissions deans who control their schools' budgets for financial aid.

In the literature they hurry to reassure dumbstruck parents that only the wealthiest families pay "the sticker price," as the published tuition figure is often called. The phrase fits, since the system allows the enrollment managers to maneuver like car salesmen. Nobody ever pays the sticker price at a car dealership either. Salesmen adjust the price depending on how badly they need to sell the car. It guarantees maximum flexibility. But even car salesmen don't have the advantages of an enrollment manager. For one thing, enrollment managers don't have to make a profit. Best of all, when they offer a student a discount on tuition—a guaranteed loan or a grant—they're in possession of all his family's financial information, thanks to FAFSA. They know just how much or how little to offer, because they know just how much the family can afford to pay.

Tuition discounting resembles the effort to downgrade the importance of SAT scores, at least in its effects, for it greatly expands the discretion of the admissions officials, enlarges their room to maneuver. A "test-optional" policy allows them to weigh more heavily the subjective factors of their own choosing—athletic prowess, legacy status, family wealth—and eliminates the opportunity for second-guessing from outside kibitzers. Tuition discounting insulates them from scrutiny in the same way. Who knows why they make the decisions they do? If none of us pays the same price, we pay just the price the enrollment manager wants us to pay, and no one but him needs to know what it is. I kept hearing that the admissions process "empowers" people. And it does: usually the people who run the college.

For the student and his family, tuition discounting nearly always entails large amounts of debt, since most offers of aid include loan packages too. Colleges have no incentive to discourage students from taking on debt; when a kid borrows money to pay for school, the school itself has no "exposure," as the bankers say. The lender—a bank or the government—holds the note, and the student assumes the liability. The colleges get the money up front.

"We're borrowing eighty billion dollars a year to go to college," Vedder said. Most of that is subsidized by the government. Two-thirds of college graduates enter the wider world with an average debt load of $22,000.

"That's the figure the establishment likes to use, anyway," he said. "Twenty-two thousand. It sounds more benign than it really is. Remember, that's the *average*. If you can't swim and you hear the river is only an average of four feet deep, you think, 'Great, I'll cross.' But that's an average. Somewhere the river is going to be six or seven feet deep, and you're gonna drown. For lots of families it's lots worse than twenty-two thousand."

The bigger the loan, the greater the chance for a default. One education researcher, Kevin Carey of the advocacy group Education Sector, calculates that one out of every five students who borrows more than $15,000 will default on the loan within ten years. And that's just for kids who graduate. More than 30 percent of college students never finish school. Their default rates are much higher.

"I have horror stories I could tell you," Vedder said. "Stories to break your heart. I've got kids with eighty, a hundred thousand dollars in debt, and no job. They went into college thinking, 'I'm doing this to invest in my future.' And of course all the messages from the adult world tell them they've got to do this. Well, if you look at higher education as an investment, there's a lot of disappointed investors out there."

I worried about those "messages" from the adult world. The availability of aid money has encouraged more people than ever to go to college. Of course the reverse might be truer: so many people want to go to college that the amount of aid money has grown to accommodate them. Whichever it is—and the question is probably a chicken-and-egg riddle that can't be solved—there's no denying that the customers keep coming. Those messages must be pretty strong to override the risks of impoverishment that come with borrowing money to buy a college degree. Ten years ago, a large majority of American parents—67 percent—believed that "there are many ways to succeed in today's world without a college degree." Now fewer than half believe that.

"The idea that you need a college education—you've just got to have one—has been getting more popular probably since Harvard opened in 1636," Vedder said. "It got a big boost with the GI Bill. Now it's really taken off. Forty years ago three percent of the mailmen in the United States had a bachelor's degree. It was a rare thing for a mailman to have a college degree—which makes sense, right? No one would claim you needed a bachelor's degree to deliver the mail. Well, it's now up to thirteen percent. We've got a lot of college-educated mail carriers. And I would submit to you that not much has changed in the way mail is delivered in the forty years that would warrant a bachelor of arts degree. Why is this? What happened?"

Talking with Vedder, I felt sometimes that I was getting to the nub of the irrationality of American college admissions—that I'd been splashing in the shallows all this time and was heading at last into the deeps. He talked about bloat and gold-plating and the downgrading of teaching. He pulled more figures from the air: over the last twenty years, the number of support staff at colleges—administrators and their helpers, mostly—has doubled; the number of instructors has risen a comparatively meager 50 percent. And most of those new teaching jobs were part-time. The average presidential salary has risen six times as fast as faculty salaries. At public four-year universities, only twenty-six cents of every dollar spent goes to actual classroom instruction. And as Bob Morse discovered, at most schools there's no way to know how much learning is going on.

"There are tests the colleges could administer to their students to find out," he said. "Give it freshman year, then senior year, before-and-after kind of thing, to see if there's improvement over the four years."

"And the schools don't want to do it," I said.

"They don't want to do it?" He shot a look at Dan and gave a little snort. "Putting it that way is much too nice. They're actively opposed to it!" He rose in his chair. "They fight it! Think about that. Here we are, educators in the most test-happy business in the world. We test for everything. Testing is what we do. We test for law degrees, grad schools, medical school. But we won't test for the one thing that affects us most. We're great believers in the dissemination of knowledge. But the one kind of knowledge we don't want disseminated is, 'Are our college students learning anything? Are we getting anything for all this money?'"

I'D ALREADY CONCLUDED THAT THE question of learning too often seemed beside the point. A college degree long ago ceased to be reliable proof of acquired knowledge. This is why, as studies show, we have college graduates who can scarcely write a complete sentence and identify John Quincy Adams as the bass player for the Funkadelics.

By the time I left Vedder's office higher education looked like a house of cards. I couldn't see what was propping it up. Surely the propaganda, all by itself, wasn't sufficient to account for our mad cultural obsession with college—propaganda like the brightly colored viewbooks, the misleading FAQs from the College Board, the earnest, endless assurances from every side that a $200,000 "investment in the future" would bring $800,000 in lifetime returns. I couldn't explain it, anyway, until my lunch with Rob.

We had nearly exhausted our complaints about our EFCs in the fog of our FAFSA fatigue. He told me I had the wrong metaphor.

"What if it's not a house of cards?" he said. "What if it's a bubble?"

Bubbles were much in the news just then. Two had popped in the last six months, with spectacular consequences. First the housing market crashed; home prices had gone up and up on a draft of high spirits and hallucinatory expectation, and then came crashing down. The stock market soon followed the same course, for the same reason: assets had been priced far beyond their real worth. Ordinary people had gone deeply into debt to invest in both on the assumption that we would reap returns that, we now saw, were never going to be realized. It did sound familiar.

"It's a giant nothing inflated on a foundation of nothing," Rob said bitterly. "Nothing but hope. No one can really say that a degree from Princeton is worth fifty-two thousand dollars a year." Princeton was his son's dream school. "The only thing that keeps that number afloat is unrealistic enthusiasm."

It was like the tulip craze, the classic bubble of econ textbooks. People fixated on a certain commodity, a bunch of flowers in this case, and through talking to one another, stoking one another's enthusiasm, became convinced that it was absurdly valuable. It was a kind of mass self-hypnosis, and it was unsustainable.

"Reality always wins out in the end," Rob said. "And here we've built huge billion-dollar industries around the belief that a college education is worth more than it is."

But how much was it worth? I didn't doubt that the lifetime earnings of a college graduate were far higher than those of someone who only got through high school. But maybe this was part of the bubble too. Most jobs, after all, even high-paying jobs, are learned on the job, not in college. What happened if employers decided that they were paying a premium for college graduates on the mistaken belief that the grads had some uniquely valuable skill over nongraduates?

I mentioned a theory I'd been reading about, held by many economists, including, I later learned, Richard Vedder. Their idea was that higher education had become a "signaling system." The system was too elaborate and highly inefficient, but it served a valuable purpose. Employment tests were effectively banned in the United States forty years ago—for good reason: some employers used test results as an excuse to deny a job to an applicant they didn't want to hire on other, illegitimate grounds, such as race or creed. The ban on employment tests was a solid blow against prejudice, but it did leave employers rather in the dark about the people they were hiring. And so, since the early 1970s, a college degree that takes at least four years to earn has performed the function of the employment test that used to take half an hour to administer.

The decline of secondary education has made this signaling function all the more important: a high school degree doesn't indicate much about the person who earns it. A college degree, on the other hand, does send a signal to an employer. It conveys information. It says that more likely than not an applicant is fairly bright, knows how to come to work on time, has some personal ambition, performs tasks without a fuss, and won't make too much trouble.

"That doesn't seem like a whole lot of information for four years at fifty-two thousand dollars a year," Rob said. Someday, he said, and maybe soon, someone would come along to establish a widely recognized credential that sent the same signal as a bachelor's degree but without the expense, and the bubble would burst. Already, in the recession that followed the crash of the housing and stock markets, community colleges and for-profit postsecondary schools were seeing a surge in enrollments from students seeking their (often) less expensive degrees.

If I hadn't just seen my 401(k) decline by 40 percent and my house lose a quarter of its value, I might not have been so susceptible to Rob's bubble talk. But it was at least conceivable if unlikely to happen any time soon: a family could pay $200,000 for an education, borrow money to finance it, and then see the degree lose half its value, collapsing under the weight of its own unreality, leaving the family with a mountain of debt while their wised-up neighbors scrambled toward much cheaper ways to acquire the marketable good that education is supposed to provide. Economic calamity has a way of dispensing with illusion.

"So here's the sensible thing to do," I told Rob. "If you're right. We should drop out of the bubble. Get our kids into a discount college. Maybe suggest they take a year off. Get them to focus on what they want to do with their lives. Stop wasting time."

"So that's what you're going to do?"

"And make them hate us for the rest of their lives?" I said. "I don't think so." I might be crazy but I'm not nuts.

8

THE WAITING

Through the keyhole — the cost of burnout —
more art than science — the interview —
the wrong sweatshirt —
the *New York Times* vs. CBS News —
drinks with Polonius — over the hump —
an unlikely letter — waiting list

THERE WAS nothing now but the waiting. A handful of people were busy determining my son's future while I was busy complaining about paying for it. My son, for his part, betrayed no emotion, at least to us. He knew as we did that it was all in the hands of the admissions committees. I had read The Books often enough, and spoken to a sufficient number of college pros, to have a good sense of what goes on behind the closed doors of the admissions office while the rest of us pace the waiting room and peer nervously through the keyhole.

The boy's life had become a file. His application had been received electronically, then printed out, and gathered into a manila folder by a small army of undergraduates hired on work-study grants. With thousands of others, his folder had been placed in the care of an admissions director, or a vice president for admissions, an assistant admissions provost, an admissions associate director, an admissions assistant director, an admissions senior associate director, an admissions counselor, or—descending the ranks precipitously—a lowly admissions liaison, perhaps a part-timer. The metastasis of titles is misleading. Whatever their position is called, they're all in the same business, sprinkling pixie dust and waving wands, dashing dreams or making them come true.

Yet it's a rough life, to hear them talk, and I don't doubt it. Admissions professionals are young and they're old, but seldom in between. In admissions offices they speak of the "missing middle." The director or dean is usually a man or woman in his fifties or older. The director is assisted by one or two deputies who are either waiting for the boss to quit or die or hanging fire until they're offered a directorship of their own at another school. Below them are another one or two associate directors, perhaps in their early forties, who've committed to a life in admissions and hope to rise in time to the level of deputy or beyond. And then comes the age gap, the missing middle: a vanished stratum, a blank in the fossil record. A large majority of employees in an admissions office are in their early or mid-twenties, only a few years out of school—often the school whose gates of admission they now guard. They're doomed to spend a few years in the business and then get the hell out.

They quit for various reasons. The pay scale is discouraging, between $30,000 to $35,000 for counselors (studies show), and salaries don't hit the high five figures until, after many years, you reach the top; a chief admissions officer who has taken on the added duty of dispensing financial aid—an enrollment manager—can sometimes break into six figures. Other reasons are more intimately personal. One former counselor told me she was sick of getting her heart broken every spring by turning down kids who had clearly lived their lives in the hope of getting an offer that she knew she couldn't make. "I'd be sick for a month after the letters went out," she said. Another told me she left for ethical reasons. "I'd lead these kids on," she said. "We'd travel from high school to high school, and go to college fairs. I'd meet kids who I knew had no chance of getting in. But it was my job to get them to apply. We needed those apps. We had to keep the acceptance rate down. It's like I was setting them up to fail."

It's burnout that most often causes the young people to quit. The admissions office recruits them from the ranks of the student tour guides, a hiring pool that guarantees large numbers of outgoing and upbeat twenty-three-year-old counselors. Beyond that the job requires a unique and maybe impossible pairing of personal traits, a love of frenetic travel along with a high tolerance for solitude. For five weeks in spring and five weeks in fall you're in constant motion, touring high schools and visiting college fairs in a rented Taurus and sleeping on scratchy sheets in the Hampton Inn. Winter comes and you metamorphose from a traveling salesman into a scholastic monk, locked in your apartment and poring over the hundreds of applicant files you've been given to read. How much time is spent on each file differs from counselor to counselor, of course. "I've heard people say they average fifteen minutes reading each essay," a sardonic ex-counselor once told me. "Unbelievable. Fifteen seconds? Believable." But there's no doubt that it is exhausting, lonely work.

The easy files are the "auto-admits" and "auto-denies." A first-generation Haitian immigrant with 2400 SATs and a 4.4 GPA from the Catholic high school where she captained the lacrosse team and ran the soup kitchen is a clear auto-admit. Auto-denies make up a much bigger group, though each can usually be identified as quickly as a clear admit: kids whose scores and grades fall below some minimal threshold, or a middling kid whose slipshod app betrays an indifference toward the school he's applying to. The third group is the in-betweens, and after their files are read—fifteen minutes or fifteen seconds, no one will ever know—the counselor writes a brief summary of the contents on a "master sheet." Then he calculates a numerical ranking based on the applicants' grades, scores, recommendations, extracurriculars, and the quality of the essay. In some schools one numeral is given each for academic credentials and personal qualities; other committees content themselves with a single combined ranking. This is likewise noted on the cover sheet. The formula used to derive the number—how much weight is given to each element in the equation—varies from school to school too. And it's always a trade secret.

The file passes to a second reader or goes straight to the admissions committee, which meets periodically throughout the season, though some committees wait till mid-March and dispatch the files in a weeks-long marathon. At the meeting the master sheet for each file is read aloud, and counselors may plead the case of a marginal applicant that has struck their fancy. Final decisions are made about admits, wait lists, and denies. By all accounts serious disputations are rare. The final authority of the director is unquestioned, for the director alone knows precisely the kinds of students the school is seeking that year as a matter of (nonpublic) policy.

There are long-term trends for the director to consider. Over the last generation, for example, many more girls than boys have been going to college. It's not unusual for girl applicants to outnumber boy applicants by three to two. Folklore holds that a sixty–forty ratio in an incoming class represents a kind of point of no return; a school acquires a reputation as a girls' school, further driving the boys away, or what's worse, it begins to attract the wrong kind of boys for the wrong reasons: male predation can become a problem. A downward spiral kicks in, or so every college president fears. The problem is all the more acute because on academic merit alone the girls are more appealing applicants. Their GPA and their verbal test scores are much higher than those of boys, on average; their essays are better written, and their records show fewer behavioral problems. When the University of California moved to a "gender-blind" admissions policy, judging applicants on the merits without regard to sex, the admit rate for girls rose to 56 percent from a rough fifty–fifty equivalence.

Whatever the reason for the gender imbalance, college administrators across the country have been going to great lengths to lasso the boys—adding sports programs, building bigger gyms, and expanding departments in engineering, math, and the hard sciences, which are historically attractive to men. And the presidents make sure their admissions directors are doing their best to "rectify" the problem of gender imbalance by lowering the academic threshold for the (mostly white) boys who apply.

Anyone who doubts the futility of human progress should ponder this. After several generations of vicious racism, followed by protest marches, civil rights lawsuits, accusations of bigotry, appeals to color-blindness, feminism, and eloquent invocations of the meritocratic ideal, the latest admissions trend in American higher education is affirmative action for white men. Just like the old days.

TALK WITH ADMISSIONS DIRECTORS AND before long—two minutes, maybe three—they will tell you their work "is more art than science." In describing how they put together an incoming class, they tend to use the verb "sculpt." They make the process sound more wide-open than it is, even in the most holistic offices. The same sardonic ex-counselor explained to me the restrictions a dean faces when sculpting his class. "Hooks are everything," she said. A "hook" is an attribute that automatically gives one applicant an advantage over another. In the incoming class at a selective school, she told me, as many as 65 percent of the admits could be hooked.

"Twenty-five to thirty percent are going to legacies," she said—the children of alumni who have built strong ties to the school through tradition, family lineage, sentiment, and large annual donations. "Another ten to fifteen have to be URMs"—underrepresented minorities. "Development cases are at least ten percent"—those wealthy kids whose parents, though not alumni, show signs of incipient generosity. "Fifteen percent of the slots go to athletes of one kind or another," she said. "Some of the schools

are big on the helmet sports—football, hockey. The teams have big
rosters. That can really drive down your SAT average. The rule of
thumb is, the better the athlete, the lower the test score." Every all-
conference linebacker with a 1300 cumulative, in other words, has
to be balanced by a Jimmy Neutron with a 2400, to keep from sliding down the page at *U.S. News.*

If two out of every three slots is "hooked," the admissions dean
has one-third of a class with which he can play Michelangelo. In an
incoming class of three thousand, he has only a thousand slots to
fill with the jazz dancers, dulcimer players, hip-hop poets, Eagle
scouts, macrobiotic chefs, yearbook editors, transgendered Republicans, manic-depressive performance artists, research biochemists,
lesbian activists, business-club go-getters, experimental screenwrit-
ers, and software dweebs whose presence will allow the dean to
brag on his famously diverse and culturally vibrant student body.
And for the unhooked applicant, the arithmetic is just as severe,
indeed despairing. The *Fiske Guide* may tell you your dream
school accepts 10 percent of applicants. One in ten is steep odds,
but maybe worth a daydream. In practice the number is probably
only a third of that, just slightly better than 3 percent. Three in a
hundred: much worse than a crapshoot.

I DIDN'T EXPLAIN ALL THESE unsettling realities to my son as I
learned them, during this period of the long wait. I compensated
for his ostentatious cool by displaying jitters enough for both of
us, with a few extra tossed in for my equally placid wife. On the
one hand, our family had, figuratively speaking, no hooks. We had
no legacy advantage to offer, no development possibilities, no athletic prowess. On the other hand, he might receive an unforeseen
affirmative-action boost from the fact of his maleness. Our neighborhood buzzed with word that a boy two blocks over had just
been admitted early decision to a highly selective liberal arts school
in Ohio, whose admissions director had said publicly she could

overlook a relatively low SAT score or GPA if otherwise qualified boys would just agree to enroll. For my son's sake I could pray for more deans like that one—until my daughter applied to college, of course, and then I would sue.

My jitters showed up under the slightest pressure. One day there was a voice mail from an admissions counselor at Georgetown, the only one of my son's hoped-for schools that required an interview. The counselor left the phone number and e-mail of a local alumna who would give him the once-over.

"Should I call her?" he asked.

"Yes," I said hurriedly.

"E-mail might be better."

"No," I said. "Call. Please. It's quicker."

A few days later, when I asked him what day he'd arranged to meet his Georgetown contact, he said he hadn't made an appointment.

"Call her," I said. "Now."

"I think e-mail might be better," he said.

"Then send an e-mail! The thing is, just do it."

I returned to my book as he tapped away at the family computer.

"Do I say 'Ms.' or 'Mrs.' or 'Miss'?" he said. "I don't know if she's married. And she might be married but still use Ms., right? What if she's a doctor?"

"Use Ms."

He composed his e-mail aloud. He had done this occasionally while working on his application essays, recasting sentences and altering word choices apparently at whim. I assumed he did it then as a way to annoy me. I didn't know why he was doing it now. Maybe he wasn't as serene as I thought.

"'Dear Ms. Young: Mr. Pels of the admissions office told me I had to get in touch with you—'"

"Mr. Pels *suggested* I get in touch with you," I called from my chair.

"That works . . . 'suggested I get in touch with you to get an interview—'"

"To *request* an interview," I said, rising from the chair and starting to move about the room.

"'. . . to *request* an interview with you . . .'"

"You don't want to say 'get in touch with you to get an interview with you . . .'"

He squinted at me.

"I'm making a suggestion," I said. "For the sake of euphony."

He went back to the keyboard. "'I stand ready to meet you whenever,'" he said, tapping.

"Stand ready?" I was looking over his shoulder. "It sounds like you're answering a ransom note. And whenever what?"

"Just *whenever*. What's wrong with that?"

"'. . . I can meet at your convenience . . .'" I prompted.

"'I can meet at your convenience whenever—'"

"No," I said.

He assumed his familiar position—forehead on keyboard—when he finished the e-mail and I insisted he run a spell-check.

"You were right, as always," he said, more defeated than angry. "I should have just called her. Calling would have been much easier. Next time I'll make sure to listen to my dad."

THE INTERVIEW WAS SCHEDULED FOR the following Saturday morning, at a Starbucks nearby. Several of his friends slept at our house the night before, following a debauch in the basement. Ping-Pong and the Xbox were implicated, but that was all I knew, or wanted to know. He emerged from below with tousled hair, a sleepy stare. He was, of course, running late. He moved in slow motion.

"You'll need to shave," I said.

"I don't need to shave," he said.

"You need to shave. And comb your hair."

I was hovering as he went about his ablutions. Ever since the apps were sent in and the waiting had begun, I had weakened in my resolve to lay off The Books and the Internet. I had torn an article out of a business magazine: "The College Interview: More Than Just Words." While he shaved I repeated what I remembered of its advice.

"Be yourself," I said.

"Okay."

"Relax," I said. "Look her in the eye, give a firm handshake, and make sure your hand is dry."

"Okay."

"Be sure to have some questions to ask her," I said. "Do you have any questions about Georgetown you could ask her?"

"Um," he said.

"Don't ask about basketball. Ask about academics. They want to know you're interested in academics. Talk about your favorite classes."

"What classes?"

"Show passion," I said, recalling the article the best I could. "And for chrissakes comb your hair."

"Why? The hat will just mess it up all over again."

"Please, please don't wear your baseball cap to the interview," I said. "Your mother would kill me."

He closed his eyes.

"Another thing. I don't mean to nag. But you say 'like' too much. 'I mean, it's, like, okay to, like, use that with, like, your friends.' But this interview could be kind of a big deal. You might want to watch that."

He didn't say anything. He could have erupted, told me to mind my own business, get off his case, but he knew that silence was a far more effective response, since it let my words hang in the air, their boorishness exposed and undeniable.

"Hell with it," I said. "Talk the way you want. Be yourself."

"You told me that already."

I handed him a paper towel to wipe the dollop of shaving cream dangling from his earlobe. "I'm late," he said, suddenly come to life. He grabbed a sweatshirt and pulled it down over his polo shirt against the chill. I made him drag the brush through his hair. He jangled his keys as he bounded off the porch. At the car door he turned and gave a reluctant wave.

"Look at your sweatshirt," I said, too loudly, with a sinking heart.

He looked at his chest.

"You're wearing a BSU sweatshirt. You're going to a Georgetown interview and you're wearing a sweatshirt from BSU."

"Not a good idea," he agreed. He yanked the sweatshirt back over his head. His hair stood up like cornstalks.

I went back to the morning newspaper and waited helplessly for him to come home.

I HAD BEEN FOLLOWING THE news more attentively than usual—international, national, financial, and collegiate. The jitters I felt were widely shared in the early months of 2009; the worst of the financial crisis had passed, it seemed, but the recession was sure to linger and likely deepen, and few experts had claimed to size up the consequences of an economic derailment so vast and complex. Education experts, unfortunately for me, were the exception. Between the application deadlines at the beginning of the year and the end of March, when decision letters would arrive, they issued periodic updates about the recession's effects on college admissions. The recession, apparently, was causing schools to . . . do everything. All at once.

The *L.A. Times* interviewed several experts, and their conclusions had that authoritative ring I had come to expect. Hard times, they said, had forced (1) more kids to apply to public colleges and universities because of the lower tuition, even though (2) loss of tax revenue was leading to tuition increases in public universities, which would cause fewer people to apply especially since (3) more of them will be drawn to private colleges which will offer generous financial aid packages although (4) the increased financial aid packages from private schools would push more students to public schools because families would be reluctant to take on more debt in a recession, and besides (5) most private schools were cutting back on financial aid because the recession had hurt their endowments. This would undoubtedly cause more kids to apply to lower-cost public schools unless it didn't.

In March the *New York Times* announced that "applications to elite colleges are up this year," a few days before CBS News came out with a story saying that "applications are down at top liberal arts schools." The recession had caused schools to extend their waiting lists, except for those schools who were shrinking their waiting lists or, because of the recession, abandoning them altogether. Hard times had forced schools to increase "merit aid" except for those schools that reduced merit aid drastically, thanks to the recession. One story said that fewer kids would be applying early decision, reluctant to commit in times of economic uncertainty; a group of college counselors issued a report advising its members to expect an increase in early-decision applicants, because the recession would force students to nail down their options early.

The same reasoning led experts to predict that the recession would have a profound effect on "summer melt," referring to the number of admitted students who send in their deposits in spring but then fail to matriculate in the fall. The recession would greatly diminish summer melt, experts said, because worried families were more likely to stick with the commitments they made; the recession would also greatly increase summer melt, as students shopped around for the best financial offers and then reneged on their original commitments at the last minute.

Needier students, needless to say, would be the hardest hit, because colleges were courting families that could pay the sticker price in full. Also, needier students would be the unexpected winners this year: the recession would cause colleges to admit more full-pays, which would free up more aid money for poorer kids. That's why the recession would hit the middle-income applicants hardest. Colleges would shift recruitment toward the higher-income and lower-income kids. Luckily for them, the middle class was sure to be the real beneficiary here. The recession would force colleges and universities to expand aid to families who were neither rich nor poor if they looked likely to boost a school's yield.

I did find one assertion that I knew was unassailably true. "This year," said the *New York Times,* "it may help, more than usual, to have a fat wallet."

HE WAS BACK FROM HIS interview in half an hour. I calculated it took ten minutes to drive to the Starbucks, ten to drive home, which left him ten for the interview.

"How did it go?"

"Good," he said.

"Didn't take very long," I said. "Not much time to make the sale."

"I guess not. She didn't really, like, have much to say."

"Well, I think the idea is that you're supposed to do most of the talking."

"Really?"

"The idea is that she's interviewing you. You weren't interviewing her."

"She was okay," he said. "It doesn't matter. I'll never get into Georgetown anyway. Never."

He sat down with the look of a beaten prizefighter and leaned back in the couch. He ran through the schools he'd applied to, offering a detailed assessment of his chances. He grabbed a finger for each one. He said he was still confident of his safety schools: Tech and Indiana University. Beyond that, he said, "I'm not optimistic." His reasoning was elaborate and highly informed. Georgetown was out. Notre Dame was out, Vanderbilt was out, BSU was out.

"Georgetown's acceptance rate keeps going down every year," he said. "It's, like, fifteen percent and falling." His SATs put him in the middle of the range for Notre Dame and Vanderbilt—and anybody at or below the middle range was in trouble, he said, since those low-score slots went to athletes and legacies, and he was neither. As a state school, BSU had to balance its class geographically, for political reasons, and it would only take so many kids from our part of the state or from any single high school. Several kids at his school who'd applied to BSU had better numbers than his. They'd be accepted before he would. BSU was out of reach.

On the upside, he might make it to UNC Chapel Hill, which was good. "They need boys," he said.

I was going to ask him how he knew all this stuff but I stopped myself. The information flows in the teenage world were beyond explanation. I thought of my attempts to push The Books on him, all to no use; I remembered how hard it had been to get him even to discuss schools. I thought of his unflappable nonchalance, how it puzzled me, and irritated me. All along he'd been absorbing most of what I was trying to learn.

He'd been more nervous than I was.

ROB AND HIS WIFE CAME over for drinks. My daughter sat at the TV, my son at the computer in the other room. March was ten days old but it still carried the late-winter death pallor. The decision letters would soon be in the mail. We tried to move on to other subjects but the conversation inevitably returned to kids and college, like a man trying to walk with one foot nailed to the floor. We kept circling back. I didn't mind. Discussing the subject with our friends could even be relaxing. I'd discovered that several of them were more neurotic than I was, and our conversations left me with the reassuring knowledge that I was not, after all, the craziest person in the country.

"Some nights I'll wake up and go over our list of schools," Rob said. "And I think, 'We blew it. He can't get into any of these. What if he doesn't get in anywhere?'"

His wife expressed her exasperation—with her son, not with her fretful husband. He's as bright and engaging as teenagers come, yet she insisted his chances had been squandered through his inattention and casual attitude. Her son's a terrific writer, she said, but his essays were dreary. He applied to schools beyond his reach (she believed); in addition to his many virtues, he has great self-assurance. She didn't want to discourage him for fear of deflating his confidence, but she didn't want him crushed either, from the steady progression of rejection letters that she was sure were soon to arrive.

In response I embarked on a discourse inspired by a recent conversation I'd had in my office. I'd been thinking it over ever since. These are wonderful kids, I told her, with every advantage in life; where they go to college doesn't matter in the long run; they are destined to live full and happy and successful lives, and if their destiny is otherwise, then no top tier school will change it.

I told her about a friend at work, who had mentioned his own wandering through the craziness. His daughter was a prize, in person and on paper: SATs in the high 2300s, a 4.0 GPA at a highly regarded public high school, a long and varied list of extracurriculars. "So I relaxed," he said. The girl's first choice was Notre Dame, her second BSU. "I thought, 'This shouldn't be a problem.'" She was rejected by both, a victim presumably of quotas for boys. Only Tech put her on the waiting list, and she was admitted late summer. That was five years ago. Now the kid is in graduate school in architecture, one of Tech's strongest departments and a field she'd never have considered before enrolling there. The initial horror— she didn't get in, even with 2360 boards!—yielded to real life and one of its most charming qualities, serendipity.

"This is our problem," I said, sliding into my Polonius mode. "When it comes to our kids, we crave certainty. And no wonder. For eighteen years all our energies have gone into giving them a settled childhood, with everything in its place, everything predictable, everything planned and hoped for years in advance. And now we can't see more than a few months ahead. The path turns a corner, disappears into the woods, and it scares us half to death.

"But all this clarity and certainty we've spent all these years cultivating, it was really counterfeit. A mirage. And now here we are back to real life. Real life is unsettled, uncertain. It's unpredictable. We should stop obsessing and just accept the uncertainty! Otherwise we're rebelling against life itself!"

At least I think that's what ol' man Polonius said. I can't recall precisely. I didn't make a note of it, because what happened next meant it no longer mattered.

Our guests were shrugging on their coats when my son appeared at the door of the living room. His face was flushed and his arms were raised in a gesture of triumph.

"I just got an e-mail," he said. "I got into Tech."

The women went to hug him. Menacing specters that had wobbled in the ether for many months crashed to earth and vaporized. He was going to college somewhere. The uncertainty vanished in an instant. I might have teared up, from relief mostly. I hate uncertainty. It drives me nuts.

"Congratulations," Rob said. "You're over the hump." The boy turned to thank him, but then he saw Rob was talking to me.

MY SENSE OF RELIEF, AND maybe his too, was genuine but short-lived. The problem with a safety school is that although it's the place you're sure you can get into, it's also the place you know you don't really want to go to. His allegiance over the last few weeks had been shifting. Notre Dame fell behind daily throughout the winter, as he checked the local temperatures in South Bend, Indiana. BSU was now at the top of the list. The shift in his thinking occurred not long before the local paper ran stories about the mounting difficulty of getting accepted at BSU. "An increasing number of students with top grades and impressive test scores"—many from our area, one article said—"are losing slots at the state's premiere schools to out-of-state students," who could afford to pay higher tuition. The article told the story of a local SuperKid. A valedictorian with a 4.01, captain of the lacrosse team, prizewinning photographer . . . "But he still couldn't get in," the reporter wrote, dumbstruck.

Then one afternoon my wife brought in the mail and held up an envelope addressed to him. "Uh-oh," she said, handing it to me. It was from the office of admissions at BSU. It was thin—wafer thin, whippet thin, rejection-letter thin. "I can't open it, can I?" I said.

"No," she said.

So I held it up to the light, turned it around and back to front and downside up, shook it stupidly, like a chimp with a graphing calculator. Under a reading lamp I could just make out the opening lines of a letter, addressed to "Mr. Ferguson." I read aloud what I could.

"The committee on admission has reviewed your application something something something I trust this will be the case with you and something encourage you to continue to challenge yourself . . ."

A kiss-off. They don't open with "We regret to inform you" anymore. Instead it's all weasely indirection. My face was suddenly very hot. I remembered how I'd felt thirty years ago, when the thin envelopes came: guilty, offended, angry, humiliated, and deeply sorry for myself. But this time was much worse, because this time it was happening not to me but to him.

He didn't get home till almost dinnertime. I heard him coming in the door. He dumped his backpack with a floor-shaking whomp, and went into his room to change. I paced around the kitchen as his mother got dinner ready. We didn't look at each other. When he emerged I told him he'd gotten a letter from BSU. "Oh God," he said. I handed him the envelope. "It's really thin," he said. He sliced it open with a thick finger.

I watched him scan the first few lines, the sentences I'd been able to pick out.

"It's okay," I said.

"No," he said, waving me off. "Please."

He read for a long time, reading and rereading. "It's from the dean of admissions," he said finally. "I'm not sure what it means, but I'm not rejected. Not yet anyway."

He handed me the letter, and I saw that the flattering first line wasn't the dean's way of letting him down easy. "Please give serious consideration to our school," he wrote, "as the place where you might continue to grow and thrive." He suggested the boy come for an overnight visit—which "students often find helpful in making their choice of the college they will ultimately attend."

There was no offer of admission, however, no flat assertion that he had been accepted to BSU.

"So are you in or not?" asked my wife.

"I don't know," my son said. "It's not a rejection letter, but it's not an acceptance letter either."

Then what was it? I'd never heard of such a thing—a nonacceptance acceptance? A nonrejection rejection? If it wasn't an acceptance then it was the work of a sadist. The dean was dealing with thousands of young people and their parents at an emotionally tender moment. Surely he knew the mildest tremor would be interpreted as an earthquake and send them running out to the street in their underwear, hysterical. A school could never send such a letter to a kid and then not make a solid offer. It would be impossibly cruel.

I was confused; therefore I became pedantic and bogusly authoritative. I improvised a little lecture on how the market worked. Admissions went both ways, I told my wife and son. There were buyers and sellers. We'd been assuming all along that we were the sellers, trying to get the schools to buy us. Suddenly the situation was reversed. We were the buyers. The letter was the work of a seller—a seller who didn't want to admit he was a seller. The admissions committee had pegged the boy as someone they were going to admit. Yet decisions couldn't be announced till the end of March. In the meantime, they didn't want some other school to grab him first. It wasn't a cruel tease, it was an act of preemption.

We took turns reading the letter. When I insisted on reading it aloud I saw my wife shake her head.

"This is cruel no matter what," she said. "This is too complicated. Why are they doing this?"

THE NEXT MORNING I DID something I hadn't done in months. I logged on to College Confidential. After some poking around I found a thread for BSU applicants and after a few moments encountered a term I'd never seen before. One of the applicants mentioned that he'd just received a "likely letter." Or at least he thought he had. "It was SO ambiguous. I read it out loud to my mom and neither of us knew what to make of it." He quoted the same letter my son had received. "So I was like . . . college confidential will know!"

And everyone on College Confidential did know. But they weren't telling, at least not in terms that a distracted parent could understand. The thread went back and forth about likely letters for quite a while before anyone asked the question most interesting to me: what's a likely letter? By way of explanation the next reply linked to a blog by an assistant dean of admissions at BSU, calling herself Dean J.

From what I could tell the dean appeared only intermittently on her own blog. Mostly it was a bulletin board for agonized applicants to BSU, gingerly submitting queries to someone who they knew held all the power. They approached her as commoners before a throne. They opened with flattery and closed with a gesture of supplication. "If I get accepted Dean J will be the first person I thank." "I will still love you and the admissions staff if I am accepted or not." "I'm glad there is someone in admissions that cares so much about students."

But the frustration was never far away. I found a thread called "Likely Letter," where the anxiety had gone viral. The applicants' posts were predictably poignant, close to heartbreaking. "Dean says the letters went out to day," one wrote. "What does the letter say?"

"Does it mean you get in?" another asked, reasonably.

Then more kids, spraying emoticons in their excitement, reported they'd gotten their likely letter. One of them added a worry: "I keep hearing horror stories of people who got a likely letter and then were rejected. Does that happen very often?" And still more kids logged on to lament that they hadn't gotten a letter. "And the wait goes on and on and on," one wrote, with a frowny face for emphasis.

After dozens of posts had stacked up and the accumulated worry was impossible to ignore, the dean decided to post a reply.

"Read past posts about these likely letters and then read the following before posting questions," she wrote in an introductory note. "Before you comment, read it again."

I did, but it didn't clear things up.

"We know time creeps by slowly between deadline and notification," she went on. "Many schools break the silence by sending 'Likely Letters' to a handful of students with strong profiles."

She made it sound as if the letters were mailed out merely as a way of killing time, a pleasant respite from the tedium that sometimes sets in after the apps are sent off. Nice of them, in a way; it certainly interrupted our tedium. But her post avoided the central question. What did the letter mean? Should it be considered maybe an "unofficial offer"? The applicants on the blog asked this same question several different ways, and got no answer.

"The letter means exactly what it says," the dean wrote. "No more no less. It is not an offer letter. We have not made any final decisions yet."

Decisions haven't been made? I couldn't help wondering, Then why send the letters? It was hard to believe that no decisions had been made yet.

She warned the recipients of likely letters not to get cocky. "There are times when mid-years arrive and show a drop in grades that prompts us to change our decision."

What decision? So decisions have been made?

"It's our way of saying we think you're a strong candidate in our pool."

Her tone swung from exasperation to condescension and back. She described the number of likely letters variously as a "handful" (ten or twelve?), "a small percentage" of the acceptances (10 percent of three thousand?), or "a very small percentage" (2 percent of three thousand?). The kids who received them could be "fairly confident" or "reasonably sure" that they "might" receive an official letter of acceptance.

She made it clear she was going to go no further in answering the question.

"Please don't call to ask about Likely Letters," she said. "They mean exactly what they say." Of course, people would only call if they were confused, and they were confused because the letters didn't say anything.

And finally, and rather pissily, she wrote:

"It is what it is."

None of the kids pressed her on the inconsistencies or rebuked her for the general sadism. I read the exchanges, if that's the word for something so one-sided. She asked them to ask questions, they bowed and shuffled and asked them, and then she pretended to answer them without answering them. Not since our Harvard tour had I seen so pure a distillation of the relationship that exists between the dean at a selective school and the kids who long to be admitted to it. The power was all on the dean's side, I thought, and she exploited it artfully. She had what they wanted.

And yet the very existence of the letter suggested this wasn't the whole story. If anything, it confirmed my pedantic lecture from the night before. A likely letter only made sense as a stratagem. The admissions committee sent the letters because they were trying to keep the kids in the corral, worried they might run off to another school before the official offer could be made. If that happened the yield would drop, and in time the school's reputation for selectivity would drop too, and so much would follow from that, so much that was not good for anyone. She couldn't admit any of this, of course, because then the kids would know: the icy self-confidence, the royal hauteur of the admissions directors, was an act. They had been as worried as the rest of us all along. They were trapped too.

BY THE TIME WE HEARD again from BSU, a few rejections had come in, along with acceptances from UNC and Villanova and a couple others, and notice from Notre Dame and Georgetown that he'd been placed on their waiting lists. These wait-list letters were frank and unillusioned; the days for leading kids on, pumping applications from students who would never get in, were over at last. While students on the waiting list are not ranked, the Georgetown dean wrote, he would enclose a card that might "give you an understanding of your possibilities." My son handed the card to me. "You can keep it for your files," he said. A box showed the percentage of wait-listed kids who had finally gotten in: .03 in 2007, .10 for 2008. "That's not three percent," my son pointed out, recalling my SAT math. "That's three-tenths of one percent." And after all my FAFSA unpleasantness, only one school offered financial aid. Villanova discounted its tuition for us from $47,000 to $42,000. I was grateful, but I wondered about the finances of parents who would find the first sum prohibitive and the second just fine.

Somehow word had gone forth among my son's friends—the natives had beat out their jungle tattoo, the kind that is silent to parental ears, that resounds only for teenagers—that BSU would officially post acceptances and rejections on its Web site at five o'clock one Thursday at the end of March. My wife and I were waiting for him when he got home from school a few minutes before five.

"Please stop hovering," he said to the twin helicopters spinning about the family computer. "Please don't stand there while I do this."

We immediately took off in different directions, my wife to empty the dishwasher, me to fidget pointlessly with the coffee-maker, both of us stealing glances over our shoulders as he sat huddled over the keyboard. We could see images swim across the screen. It went white, then filled with blue. An interesting choice of color palette. He looked for a button down at the bottom and clicked.

"It says 'Congratulations,'" he said. "I got in." I swallowed hard. My wife and I hugged, and she hugged him. I thought of hugging him too but then thought better of it; I clapped him on the shoulder and told him how proud I was, that he would never know how proud.

As we got ready for bed that night, my wife said: "The wonderful thing is, he's going to college! The terrible thing is, oh God, he's going to college."

HE LEFT TWO DAYS LATER on a weeklong school trip, a kind of farewell to life as a high schooler. We were having a cold spell, and in his absence I closed off his bedroom. I went in there one morning to find a book I'd lent him. With the shades drawn and the heat off, the room was as cool and dark as a tomb. Everything was right where he left it the morning of the trip, as if he'd rushed out the door a moment before; sneakers upside down on the floor, socks higgledy-piggledy, bed unmade, books at odd angles on the shelves. On the walls were maps he'd once studied for a geography bee in junior high. There was a framed autograph from Cal Ripken, and a caricature drawn of his ten-year-old self by a cartoonist at a summer fair. Overlapping scraps of paper were pinned to his bulletin board, mementos in sedimentary layers, ticket stubs, school pictures, box scores of games I'd forgotten filled in with little-boy lettering. A scrum of sports trophies crowded the top of his bookshelves. Above the doorsill a horseshoe was braced, a keepsake from a week we'd spent at a dude ranch the summer before sixth grade.

I sat on his bed looking at it all as I would a cluttered collection in a museum, too big and heavy a jumble for me to take in, the accumulations of a childhood that was now drawing to a close. I sat for a long time in the cool and the quiet, and then closed the door behind me, with no thought of my book.

9

In the Kingdom of the Kids

What a parent doesn't know—
orientation then and now—mining the quarry—
witchcraft and postmodernism—one dorm, two views—
the starch symphony—the perilous parking pass—
lost footing—a final surprise

"MOST OF what you can do you've already done," a friend of mine said. We were in a skylit restaurant, fresh flowers on the table, seeming more spring than the beginning of the end of summer. "From now on you're pretty much limited to writing checks, assuming you can."

We were talking about parenthood. His own children were grown and long out of college. He'd told me a story about his son. Thirty years ago or more, when his son was very young, they had tried out a new cassette recorder by listening to a spoken-word tape of "Babylon Revisited," F. Scott Fitzgerald's story from the 1930s about a divorced and dissipated writer trying to put his life together after the wild ride of the Roaring Twenties. He lost his money in the stock market crash, the character says at the story's close. "But I lost everything I wanted in the boom."

Now my friend's son is a stockbroker, making fancy money

and surrounded by other people making fancy money, a lot of them blowing it on things—drugs and drink, mostly—that put them at risk of losing other things that, someday, they will truly want, the things that matter. My friend's son told him the Fitzgerald line comes back to him day by day, thirty years later, as a reminder of what counts and how easily it can be lost.

"Now, here's what's interesting," my friend said. "I'd forgotten all about the story, listening to it, it was so long ago. But it's something he'll never forget. It shows how powerful we are as parents. What's nothing to you could be everything to them—some trifling event that you'll never remember might be a turning point in how they see the world. They don't miss anything, especially when they're very young. But you've got no way of knowing what will stick. It might be a casual remark in the car driving them someplace."

My son was about to leave home for college, and my daughter was not far behind. A phase of life—the most important part of it, the years of rearing children—was coming to an end. All along the stakes had been very high, a fact I didn't dwell on once I began my life as a parent. If parents thought too much about it, we would work ourselves into paralysis, afraid to make a wrong move or utter a misbegotten syllable.

"And after a while it's too late," my friend said. "Once they leave—and he's leaving soon, isn't he?"

A few weeks, I said.

"Once they leave, they never really come back. Not really. Not even if he graduates with a degree in art history and God forbid wants to move back home and sleep on a futon in your basement. In some essential way he's gone for good."

He smiled and stretched his arms forward in a futile gesture: "Beyond your grasp!"

I TOLD MYSELF WE'D MAKE the most of these final weeks. But before summer could tip into the pleasant languor of early August we received a summons from BSU, requiring parent and child alike to attend two days of "orientation."

I vaguely remembered something called "orientation" from my own freshman year. It consisted of dropping my suitcase on a mattress in an empty dorm room, rifling my new roommate's collection of LPs, and going downstairs to an all-dorm dinner with a Hawaiian theme, meaning we ate slices of ham topped with syrupy chunks of pineapple by the light of a pair of tiki lamps, which were included as a festive touch even though it was five o'clock in the afternoon. There was beer and a brief, uncomfortable talk from our dorm's head resident adviser, who recited obligatory counsels about the dangers of drunkenness, followed by more beer. The next morning I was assumed to be orientated, though I was merely hungover; and college began.

Such spare informality would be unthinkable today. A friend had sent me a recent article from the *Boston Globe* describing freshman orientation in 2008. At Northeastern University it lasts eleven days. Tufts' orientation went for six, and Amherst's for eight. Freshmen were treated to sightseeing bus tours, harbor cruises, karaoke nights, yoga lessons, carnivals, banquets on the quad, picnics in the woods, athletic competitions, even, once in a while, a meeting with a professor or faculty adviser to talk about school. It was a cross between a coronation festival and sleepaway camp. Every instant was packed tight with a planned activity. "We want to make sure they are constantly feeling welcomed," explained the orientation coordinator at Tufts. The important word was "*constantly.*"

As a state school, BSU couldn't afford the round-the-clock pampering. But the deans knew that some kind of student orientation, a formal introduction to the new life of college, has become obligatory; higher-education customers simply expect it, like the enormous hot tub in the gym or the bowl of complimentary condoms on the reception desk at the Wellness Center. BSU's compromise was to hold a brief orientation a few weeks before the kids moved in and classes began. And they made parents come along too.

THE DRIVE DOWN TO COLLEGETOWN gave us the first span of unin-terrupted time we'd had together since the summer began; most days I'd left for the office before he woke up and by the time I returned he was at work or off with friends. The interstate took us—lifted us, is how it felt to me—from city to countryside in the familiar stages, through the dense suburbs thinning out to the exurbs, where the Targets and Best Buys are surrounded by acres of shadeless parking lots, and then to the outskirts of the exurbs, past the Stuckey's and Cracker Barrels, and then a little farther on, to where we could glimpse from the roaring highway the quiet orchards and tumbledown barns against the distant hills. By the time we turned off to the state road that would lead us to BSU, we had struck up a conversation in a man-to-man mode. We fell to talking about his high school years, a topic for two men to reflect upon, rather than merely as father and son.

"I liked almost everything about it," he said; his teachers, his classes, his coaches. He has a gift for happiness. The nerves and agi-tation of the last eighteen months had obscured it, in part, and now, with all that behind him, and as we passed from the city where he'd spent his childhood into the countryside where his adulthood would begin, the gift revived. He told stories about friends I never knew he had. "If college is half as good as high school," he said, without finishing the sentence.

When we got to Collegetown we dropped our bags at the hotel and went looking for a restaurant and an early dinner.

Twenty years ago, you could tell without much trouble where the town began and the campus ended. That was twenty-five years ago. More to the point, that was hundreds of millions of dollars in higher-ed spending ago. Like most university towns, in the early years of the last century Collegetown welcomed the presence of the school as a touch of class and an economic boon. Now the town serves mostly as a quarry that the university mines for the material of its own expansion. Block after block of residential real estate has been sub-sumed into student and faculty housing; the university hospital—the "medical health center," which is the new word for hospital—is the town's largest individual employer and has overtaken not only the commercial center but remade the town's economy as well.

The parasite having consumed the host, the downtown looked pale and hollowed out, as though a strong wind would level the storefronts. The most basic amenities have been squeezed out—no grocery store, no hardware store, only a bare-bones drugstore—as it's filled with bars and T-shirt shops. The restaurants are of two kinds, mainly, one serving pizza slices and sopping subs on slips of wax paper, the other, gluten-free wheatberry remoulade driz-zled over a bed of house-cured caramelized shallots and emulsified Monterey Bay sea smelt. Spaced among them are a couple of white-tablecloth restaurants, where parents in from out of town feed the college kids roast beef and baked potatoes and an occasional vege-table.

We chose one of these and settled at a table outside, facing a line of empty shops set off against a reddening sky. Our conversation was easy, partly because I resisted my many dad impulses and beat down the paternal gorge when I sensed it rising. I was reminded again of his keen eye for detail. He knew the BSU football sched-ule for the fall, and the team's won–loss percentage last year, and the astonishing stats of the school's championship soccer team. He could tell me the distance between the BSU campus and other schools that old friends were attending, and how long each route would take to drive. Yet the eye, while keen, was selective. When I asked him the course requirements for the major he said he was interested in—international relations—he drew a blank. The school itself, of course, placed no strict curricular demands on students in the liberal arts.

"Have you decided on classes for this fall, then?"

"I don't know," he said. "Isn't that what orientation is for? I guess I'll have time to figure it out tomorrow."

I started to say something, stopped, then started to say something else, and finally fell silent. Classes? What classes? Suddenly it seemed impertinent for me even to address the topic, hopelessly retrograde. Ever since my talk with Richard Vedder, I'd been chewing over the signaling theory, this idea that a college degree serves mostly to transmit to an employer certain favorable information about a potential hire. I didn't like the utilitarianism of it. At the start, in the old world of Europe, higher education had been conceived in almost spiritual terms, as a way to instruct maturing minds in the treasures of civilization, the guiding ideas, the political and moral philosophies, the works of art and literature that made us what we are. Signaling theory reduced it to a preparation for workadaddy employment—time-consuming, inefficient, and expensive. And many colleges and universities were going along with it, by no longer requiring general courses that might make higher education more than a job-training program. In place of the requirements was a "do-it-yourself curriculum."

BSU offered an excellent example, I discovered. You could get a degree in the humanities without studying literature, or a degree in history without ever sitting through a survey class in American or European history. Instead of taking, say, "The History of Modern Europe," history majors could satisfy their Euro requirement by taking "Witchcraft" or "Modernity, Postmodernism, and History" or any number of seminars thrusting them into a scholarly silo built by a history professor: "Mercantilist Identities in Industrial Britain, 1895 to 1902," let's say, or "Incantations and Charms from Chaucer to Spenser." There were good professional reasons for the silos; all the incentives for tenure-track instructors pointed toward hyperspecialization. But were these the only two alternatives that higher education could offer—mere professional training on the one hand, or a patchwork of academic obsessions on the other?

I'd raised the subject with the Kitchen People and been unable to rouse much interest. No one had firm ideas about the course of study their kids should pursue. Very odd! We had struggled and sweated and risked our financial futures to get our kids into just the right school, devoted hundreds of hours and thousands of dollars to achieving the goal, and then, once the kid was admitted and the task was accomplished, we withdrew from the field. I'd had hundreds of conversations about how to get kids into college, only a handful about what they would do once they got there.

At dinner, as he wolfed down a flank steak and I stabbed at a piece of fish, I decided at last to say what I wanted to say, what he didn't particularly want to hear. The university wouldn't tell him the surest way to develop his talents, but I would. I told him he had a few precious years to take advantage of an opportunity that would never come again. Later on he could plunge into the silo, where the learning might be deep but was also cripplingly narrow. For now he should widen his lens, absorb the broader, lower-level classes first, pick up a far-ranging, general knowledge—that was still possible at BSU, I supposed. This had been the method of liberal education for hundreds of years.

"I'll keep that in mind," he said, unconvinced.

BEFORE NIGHT FELL WE DROVE through the campus to the outermost periphery. BSU follows the centrifugal pattern of the big university campus: the oldest and prettiest acreage lies in the center, where the ancient trees shade the charming old brick buildings and the quadrangles are crisscrossed with paths of paving stones, and radiating outward are buildings slightly less graceful, more sparing in ornamentation and grace notes and where the trees are a generation younger, out to the farthest reaches, to the campus version of sprawl, where the trees are upright twigs and dorms and gyms and stadiums loom like box stores, sitting shadeless in parking lots that spread out to embankments of dying grass.

The photographers seldom venture out here to take their pictures for the viewbooks. Out here, however, was where he would live and spend most of his time, in a dorm that betrayed scarcely a thought on anyone's part for warmth or visual interest. Neither porticoes nor columns nor shutters nor pediments distract from the grim duty of pack 'em and stack 'em. I drooped when I saw it. As an architectural statement, his dorm said: *DMV, Provo, Utah, 1972.* We were on the hem of a great romantic episode in his life, a time for wonder, and yet his dreary new home seemed designed to discourage all romance, to defeat all sense of wonder.

When we pulled up closer, the thing swelled in its ugliness. And he said, with an edge of excitement, "Sweet!" The dorm was locked up for the summer. He asked me to turn into a service alley to get a better view, and I nosed the car past the Dumpsters and utility boxes. He craned his neck to get a glimpse beyond the Jersey wall, guessing which window might be his. "I think that's it," he said. "Oh yes. Very sweet."

We were looking at the same building, but from different prospects, and we were seeing different things.

THE WAKE-UP CALL DIDN'T COME from the front desk the next morning. I shook off the Ambien from the night before and reached over to the next bed to jog him awake, and he uttered an expletive and moved with a swiftness I'd rarely seen from him. Evidently he thought something important was happening at last. He was dressed and down in the lobby gobbling the "complimentary free continental breakfast buffet" by the time I was through shaving.

The hotel was booked with families here for orientation, and in the hallways was a sight I'd known from years of family road trips: wandering fathers, expelled from their cramped motel rooms where the kids squabbled among the heaped sheets, and Sponge-Bob blared from the TV, each of the kids taking a turn behind the closed bathroom door, and leaving no place for Dad. So they duck down corridors, these dads do, and circle the lobby, their complimentary copies of *USA Today* tucked under their arms, looking for a public bathroom where they might lock the stall door and be alone, at peace, with their sports page. I'd been one of them many times myself. It was like seeing old friends.

Where did this misnomer, "continental breakfast," come from? No one from the Continent could choke down a breakfast like the ones offered in the little yellow-and-tan rooms off the lobby of the low-end American hotel. My son was tucking in at a table near the TV, in the blare of a cable-news morning show. From the plastic bread boxes and the wicker baskets lined with paper napkins he'd managed to assemble a boundless teenage breakfast, a symphony of starch and sugar; a hillock of biscuits, a palmful of blueberry mini-muffins, a couple toaster waffles, and three slabs of toaster French toast, rising through the surface of a lake of Mrs. Butterworth, overbrimming the Styrofoam platter; all of it washed down, horribly, with orange drink.

I made do with a bowl of off-brand quasi-Cheerios.

"You're nervous," I said.

"I'm nervous," he agreed.

"Good thing it hasn't affected your appetite."

"You should never get nervous on an empty stomach," he said.

We drove past the football stadium to a barnlike structure where registration was held. The parking lot was a demolition derby of absurdly large vehicles, driven by jumpy parents angling for a parking space. They'd stop abruptly and the doors would swing open to disgorge the kids. I dropped off my son and told him to run ahead to sign in. I parked illegally and hurried inside before I could get caught by an officious campus cop who was strutting between the cars with the air of an authority he didn't have. Inside, queues were forming alphabetically in front of folding tables, a small cordon reining in the cheerful chaos. The scene was surprisingly familiar. This was the college experience I remembered, from before the digital age: folding tables, metal chairs, scuffed floors under a ceiling of corrugated tin; bewildering queues leading who knows where, though you knew when you got there someone would ask you to fill out a form and hand you another stack of paper.

We parents mingled near the door, by punch bowls filled with lemonade and trays of shortbread cookies. We were holding ourselves back, trying to keep a single eye on our children, as inconspicuously as we could.

"I guess we're not supposed to help them, right?" one of the parents said.

"Oh no," said another. "Not if you want them to come home with you after orientation."

"This is all theirs," another parent said. "All we can do is watch. A whole new world. We're not in Kansas anymore, Toto."

I saw that my son had made it to the front of the *F*s. He was being spoken to by two student volunteers. They were piling paper on him, layering him in booklets, campus maps, lists, forms, brochures, folders, instruction sheets, a tote bag, a souvenir backpack, loading him up with the carelessness of a dowager handing luggage to a bellboy. He looked dazed. Suddenly I remembered an important piece of information I'd picked up a week earlier from an orientation letter. "Registration will be the only chance for your son or daughter to pick up a . . ."

I hurried up through the queue, pressing against his future classmates, who parted at this bizarre interruption. I reached out and grabbed his shoulders from behind. "Parking pass!" I said. "This is our only chance. Tell them to give you a parking pass!" His two counselors looked from him to me and back again. The invincible good cheer left their faces, replaced by condescension and annoyance. I was the only person over the age of twenty-two within a radius of twenty feet. I had forced myself into territory where students ruled, penetrated their colony, flashing my Dadness like a sheriff's badge. I had injected myself into a kingdom of kids. I could feel my son's shoulders shrink under my touch. The top of his ears reddened. He didn't turn around.

"Otherwise we'll get parking fines," I said to the back of his head, feebly. "Parking tickets, with fines. Wherever we park. We need a parking pass."

He nodded abruptly, muttered "I'll handle it" through tightened lips, and I knew at once, of course, the grotesque breach of etiquette I'd committed. To the kids, including him, it must have looked as though I thought I was shepherding a trembling five-year-old through the milk line on his first day of kindergarten. I don't think it had hit me quite so hard till then. This tin barn, these tables and chairs, this campus, the stadiums and the greensward crossed with walkways, this wasn't a place for parents but for their children, who would soon enough no longer be children. And I was treating him like a child.

We really weren't in Kansas anymore. "Begone," I could hear the good witch Glinda say with a wave of her sparkling wand, shooing away the Wicked Witch of the West. "You know your power is no good here."

I'D LOST MY FOOTING. ALL summer, and more and more over the last eighteen months, I was uncertain when to insert myself into his affairs, when to hold back, when to treat my son like a ward and when to welcome him as a peer. Parent orientation didn't help. While our children were off at their own sessions, we parents gathered on the old campus in a grand nineteenth-century auditorium under a barrel ceiling. A cast of deans and subdeans and directors and subdirectors took turns behind the podium, hammering a pair of themes.

We had to reconcile ourselves to our children's independence, the dean of students said. Trust that we had endowed them with the good judgment that would allow them to make fruitful use of their newfound freedom. "It can be painful," he said, "but this is the time for letting go."

Also, we had to remember that these kids were so ill-prepared for the real world that we had better intervene *right now*, before they left for good and it was too late.

"You need to have a tough conversation with your student

215

about sexual assault," the dean of students said. Young men need to know what it means. Young women need to know how to say no. Both need to learn when no means no. And then, he went on, "you need to take the time to have a candid conversation about alcohol and dependency."

A director from the finance office took the podium. "Please, parents," she said, "talk to your kids about money. Let them know the importance of a credit report. Tell them what can happen if they overdraw their checking account. Warn them about the consequences of missed payments on their credit cards."

One after another they came, telling us what to tell our children. Students should be alert to the telltale signs of depression and how to seek counseling. Always park in a well-lit spot, the police advised. Kids should use the buddy system and follow the lighted paths when walking at night. "You need to sit down with your son or daughter and draw up an emergency preparedness plan," said the representative from the emergency preparedness office. She told us the BSU campus—landlocked though it was in a little valley like Shangri-la—was particularly vulnerable to catastrophe. She mentioned "high wind storms" in particular.

She held up the school's emergency guidelines. A copy would be issued to each new student, she told us. "Make sure they post this in their rooms," she said, tapping the page. "And make sure they write down their dorm name and room number right here, in the corner. It sounds like a little thing, but it's extremely important. If they do have to dial 911 from their rooms, they'll be able to look at the guidelines and know at once where they are." She shook her head. "You'd be surprised how often they forget."

A pair of undergraduates were brought out to perform a skit. It was a playful one-act about the befuddled relationship between student and parent. The actors went through their episodic phone calls with their mothers and fathers, from the first day of school to final exams. Student life, in their portrayal, was a slacker's dream. They gorged on take-out pizza and day-old burritos, stayed up till dawn and slept till noon, blew homework assignments and missed classes, juggled credit cards and overdrafts, and fell into and out of romantic entanglements with whipsaw emotional consequences. Occasional reference was made to schoolwork, usually as an irritant or unwelcome distraction. The lesson for the parents was that the wisest course was to keep their mouths closed and their checkbooks open.

The skit was very lighthearted and cleverly performed, and it got lots of laughs from the parents who were about to spend $20,000 a year so their children could slip into this new life. I laughed along too until I thought . . . wait a minute.

But the deans rushed ahead. Absent a felony, they said, the campus police would be forgiving. The student clinic was generous and discreet, and every facility was a model of state-of-the-art, hassle-free convenience; the new gym had a vast hot tub, adjacent to its Mediterranean-size pool, and new laundry machines were being installed that would e-mail students when their clothing was dry so they wouldn't have to remember to check on their own.

"Look," the dean of students said, in a kind of summary, "they'll screw up. It's inevitable. Ninety-nine percent of the time there won't be any consequences if they do." He wanted us to know that because of BSU's system of safety nets, our children, though they may very well become narcoleptic, overfed, helpless, rutting young drunks, wouldn't end up in jail or the bughouse.

In my many months of thinking about my son's future college experience, I thought I had exhausted all the probabilities and scenarios. Now the officials at BSU were raising one more that I'd neglected to consider: his college years might be as reckless, wasteful, and thrilling as mine. I would have to put up with it.

THE WEEKS WOUND DOWN. LATE in August, on the Thursday evening before "move-in day"—as the school called it; "move-away day," as I thought of it—he and I held a final nostalgic

217

viewing of our favorite family movie, *Godfather II*. For American men, especially the denatured fathers of the suburban middle class, the *Godfather* movies act as a binding agent, letting us partake of a manliness that we have otherwise lost in changing the diapers, setting the table, and driving the minivan to the garden center to pick up a tray of fuchsias for our wives. We greet each other with lines from the movie as though we're exchanging passwords: "In my home!" one might say. "Where my wife sleeps," says another; "where my children come and play with their toys!" finishes the third. *Godfather II* is central to the native customs of my people. I have initiated my son into this knowledge.

So that night we sat in our living room, in the sepia glow of the cinematographer's palette, watching Michael Corleone save his family by destroying it, and as with all great works of art, the movie suddenly disclosed to me new facets of my own obsession. Michael Corleone himself, of course, is a college dropout, having disappointed his father by enlisting in the army and fighting the Nazis. To make amends he shoots a crooked New York police lieutenant in the neck. The only college boy to play a large role in the saga is the misfit lawyer Tom Hagen. Tom is balding and feckless and wears buttoned-up sweaters. The lesson was obvious, at least to me. Higher education saps the primal masculinity that drives American commerce and competitiveness; four years in college, three more in law school, and you will never have what it takes to be a wartime consigliere.

Yet I had deflected so many obvious lessons over the last two years that I had no trouble ignoring another one. This was the life we had chosen, to paraphrase Hyman Roth, even if it sometimes seemed that it had been thrust upon us, to paraphrase Shakespeare. College was simply built into our life as the next, inescapable phase, a fait accompli.

It was hard to read how he was reacting to this reality as it charged toward us, mere hours away. Occasionally, like my wife and me, he seemed oblivious to the inevitable, as though life was going to continue unchanged and unimpeded, humming along as it always had. I didn't know whether his obliviousness, like ours, sprang from a strategy of avoidance or from, well, obliviousness, the general mental fog that characterizes most of those who are eighteen and male. Whichever the case, when the new reality presented itself to him, it seemed to draw him up short.

"We're almost out of soda," he announced the day before we were to drive him to BSU.

"What do we need?" my wife asked.

"Coke," he said.

"But you're the only one who drinks Coke," my wife said.

"That's right," I said. "What do you care? You're going to be gone."

I said it too coldly and he looked at me as if I'd flicked the words at him.

"Oh yeah," he said. "I'll be gone."

WE'D COME BACK FROM VACATION two days before, leaving ourselves only ninety-six hours to pack him up. It was likely our last family vacation, at least in the current configuration; in the future he would want summer jobs elsewhere, and soon my daughter would be lost to college life too. So I broke off a chunk of our savings and signed us up for a cruise I'd found at half price, ten days on the sea with frequent ports of call. I'd never been on a cruise, never particularly wanted to be on a cruise, but it offered enough of what my daughter and son appreciated—a variety of activities undertaken amid a sameness of sun and water, with a hint of colorful novelty into the bargain. The planning was a welcome distraction in the last weeks, and once we were aboard there were moments of great family warmth, even giddiness sometimes, and occasionally of illumination. I caught glimpses of him as he drifted away. I learned his tricks, some of them anyway, in the forced confines of a big boat circling a closed-in sea.

One afternoon we stood together at the railing of the ship, the spray rising from several stories below.

"The water is so blue," I said. "Just like the guidebooks said. I've never seen a blue quite like that."

"That's true," he said. "It's incredible."

I speculated on the cause. Maybe it was the depth of the ocean floor, perhaps the play of the air on the water's surface. It might be the unrefracted light from a cloudless sky or an upshining from submerged coral.

"I couldn't tell you," he said.

I fell silent, and after a minute he spoke again.

"Wow," he said. "Look at how blue the water is."

I stared at him.

"I just said that," I said.

"You did?"

"Yes, and you agreed with me."

"I did?"

"Yes."

"Oh. I guess I wasn't really listening."

"Do you do that a lot?"

"Well, yeah. I guess so."

"Great."

"Not on anything important! I always listen to you if it's important."

"How can you tell it's important if you aren't listening?"

"You look different if you're saying something important."

It came out that he responded to subverbal cues—the tone of my voice or the severity of my scowl. Hearing the depth of a sigh or glimpsing the lift of an eyebrow, he could, he told me now, select the appropriate catchphrase from a small repertoire. Then he would say it—"That's weird—I see what you mean—That's terrible—Incredible—Whoa—That's great—That's true"—and knowing I was appeased, he could continue thinking his own thoughts.

"How long have you been doing this?"

"A long time," he said.

"Great. I'm pouring out my wisdom, making wry or witty observations, drawing attention to obscure truths, and my son doesn't consider it worth listening to."

He had the grace to look slightly sheepish.

"But I do appreciate your candor," I said.

He nodded. "That's true," he said.

After this a new pattern of family life began to assert itself, a subtle redistribution of weight.

MORNING BREAKS. WE DISEMBARK FOR the day and notice that today's port of call looks a lot like the port of call from the day before. I'm too cheap to hire a taxi into the heart of the city, so we walk from the docks under a bright, baking sun, armed perhaps with a guidebook and a folding map handed out aboard ship.

And thus in the heat and with growing physical discomfort I find myself in a position I know from many years' experience, from many sightseeing vacations past, arriving with my family in more American cities than I can name. It's almost a tradition, my leading the family on foot down glaring urban avenues roaring with traffic, along sidewalks so narrow we have to walk single file, where a misstep would tilt any of us into the rush of steel and rubber and fumes and certain death. We are in pursuit of a historical site, a notable church, a public building of some renown, or a museum that's come highly recommended, it doesn't matter.

None of us can hear any of the others for the traffic. The sun beats down and the heat shimmers up from the pavement, and after a few intuitive turns I am lost, though the wife and children don't know it yet. They follow expectantly, in the mistaken belief that Dad has some vague conception of where he is. The cars belch exhaust and the map dangles from my fist as we walk, loose in my grip like the battle flag of a defeated general. For years I could lead these expeditions without sacrificing my air of authority and

221

reputation for paternal infallibility. And yet now our recent trips, including our college tours of the summer before, have raised doubts in the maturing minds of the children: *He's faking it. He doesn't know where he's going.*

"It's this way," I say to them, pointing confidently.

"Are you sure?" my daughter says now.

The traffic roars. It's a question she never would have asked two years ago.

"We've been that way before," my son will say. "That's how we got here in the first place."

"It's this way," I repeat. An irritated toss of my head.

The sun beats down. A cool trickle slides down between my shoulder blades.

"Are you sure, Daddy?" my daughter says, wanting to believe.

"We're going in circles," my son says.

For the first time the murmurs of sedition inflate into full mutinies, until soon they become commonplace, with even my wife dissenting, and rather than hold on to my authority, Queeg-like, I concede—I hand over the map, find a shady spot for rest, in the end call for a cab.

My son has a truer sense of direction than I do, he can read a map with greater ease than I. In this matter, as in others, I feel the tectonic plates move, I hear a groan from the center of the earth. His authority rises as mine ebbs. Sometimes he and I strike off on our own. I notice when we do that he walks a few paces behind.

Please don't do that, I tell him.

I guess I'm like a sheepdog, he says. I want to make sure I don't lose you.

ON MOVE-IN DAY IT RAINED. Packing boxes were stacked by the door and spaced through the living room like stepping-stones in a stream of backpacks, duffels, plastic shelving, bags of cookies, suitcases, and, to complete the garage-sale scene, a toaster. One box held school supplies. His mother had been trying to keep busy by trawling the discount stores. There were manila folders, a hole puncher, a stapler, stacks of typing paper, a pencil sharpener, a twenty-four-count box of Bic pens, a clipboard, all of them looking anachronistic, artifacts from our generation rather than his. Does anybody use hole punchers anymore? Another box held his football and his basketball—the one we bought him when he began high school, caked in mud but still in commission. A pair of baseballs, resting on his mitt and batting glove. A rolled-up beach towel. A carton of Gatorade, to fill the mini-refrigerator we'd rented for his room. The dog sniffed, licked, then sniffed again, wondering what's up, sensing betrayal.

The drive was quiet. We found his dorm, double-parked once more, and carried our loads in the rain. When we were almost done he mentioned again the trouble he'd had registering for the classes he wanted.

"It's a big school," I said. "Just what you were looking for—big sports teams so you can paint your chest. Classes fill up fast."

Even his first choice for his single freshman requirement, a writing class, was filled, and so were his second and third choices.

"So what do you do now? You've got to take a writing class."

"There are three writing classes still open," he said. "I've got to pick one. One is 'The 1960s,' a sort of history course. And 'AMC's *Mad Men* and American Life,' about the TV show. And the other one is 'Intro to Queer Theory.'"

I was going to say something, release the rising gorge, but the moment passed.

"I'm sure you'll figure it out," I said.

HE LOOKED BEWILDERED WHEN WE left him, wondering what he was supposed to do with all the empty boxes. We needed gas for the drive home. I found a gas station not far from the dorm, at the edge of campus. I tried not to talk, and I thought I caught my wife giving me sidelong glances. I pulled up to the pump, slid the credit card in the slot, and shoved the nozzle in the tank of the family van. The nozzles were different down here, I noticed, far from the environmental regulations of the big city. That's one thing they get right anyway. You could shove them in cleanly, all the way, without waggling that bulky rubber sleeve and worrying that the nozzle would slip out.

My sadness, grief almost, flamed up, insanely, into anger at all the things a man can't control. I stood at the open door of the van under the dripping eve of the portico. I started to mention an anecdote I recalled, I don't know why, from his first day in kindergarten, long, long ago. In the backseat my daughter rolled her eyes.

"Stop it," my wife said to me. "I told myself I wouldn't start blubbering but I will if you keep this up."

"All right. I'm just trying to acknowledge that this is the end of something. An important part of our life just ended."

"It's the end of something but it's also the beginning of something else, something wonderful."

"To make an end is to make a beginning." T. S. Eliot. I learned that in college. I didn't buy it then either.

"No," she said. "This is a moment we should be proud of. We did it. We did it. We raised him to be a strong, kind, happy, self-confident young man, and we succeeded. It's what we were supposed to do. If you want to sulk because we did what we were supposed to do, and we did it well, go ahead. But I refuse. And don't do it around me."

She was right and I knew it, or I thought I knew it, and in time I might even come to believe it. For the moment I would sulk. I got in and slammed the door. I turned the key and when the engine roared I gunned it, until I felt a sickening tug and heard the sound of sheet metal being ripped from welded bolts, because I'd left the nozzle in the tank.

AFTERWORD

IT WAS several days before we heard from him, aside from a pair of the briefest text messages, with the obligatory typos, which provided the only evidence we had that he was still alive. At last he called late one Sunday afternoon. My wife was at the store and I lay drowsily on the sofa, watching our local baseball team get beat again—by the Phillies, again. I saw his name on the caller ID. My son's first phone call from college! After a quick hello he asked anxiously for his mother. I told him she wasn't home but I was sure I could help. He said he didn't have much time. There was a line of people behind him growing impatient. I asked where he was and he said he was in the laundry room of his dorm.

"Which goes in the hot water, colored stuff or white stuff?" he said. "Mom told me and now I can't remember."

I didn't say anything.

"And nobody here seems to know either."

I still didn't say anything.

"Or can I just put it all in at the same time? I don't understand why I can't just dump everything in all at once. I'm glad you think it's funny. It's not. I really need to know now."

This has been our only crisis, so far. He managed to avoid *Mad Men* and Queer Theory and enroll in the History of the Sixties, where he read the Port Huron Statement and learned about the valor of Abbie Hoffman from an instructor whose enthusiasm was greatly increased by virtue of his being too young to have seen any of it firsthand. I wondered whether *Mad Men* might not have been the better deal but kept my mouth shut.

He came home at Thanksgiving, and then at Christmas, and the old routines and patterns easily reasserted themselves, though not completely, of course—my aged friend in the restaurant had been right about that. Some part of them is gone for good; it's been turned away from home and toward a place we don't really see, that a parent can't reach, is not supposed to reach.

Along with the end there were several beginnings, as my wife, with T. S. Eliot's help, had insisted. Our son began his new phase of life and we began a new phase of ours, as roosting birds with a half-empty nest, and our daughter, accepting as much fatherly help as I could get away with, began her own college search. Already a few parts of the process had changed. *U.S. News & World Report* finally expired as a paper magazine, though Bob Morse and his rankings soldier on, making money and annoying the establishment. FAFSA, thanks to the Obama administration, seems to have been made marginally less confusing. Otherwise the sequence has been much the same, and just as daunting as it appeared to me the night I first met Kat Cohen: the PSAT, the test prep, the SAT, The Books and the guides, the tours, and looming up ahead, stretched along the horizon like a naval blockade, the apps and the essays and then the waiting—but calmer, much calmer. Every time we talk to my son or visit him, my daughter or my wife or me, and see the happiness and good cheer, we are all of us reminded that the effort and anxiety was a small price to pay (the tuition, however, is another story). Anyway, the process is easier this time because I know how it ends—and it's a happy ending made all the happier by my (tardy!) understanding that it's not an ending at all.

—March 2010

ACKNOWLEDGMENTS

MANY OF the people who guided me through the admissions industry and tried to illuminate the world of higher education in general are professionals who weren't crazy about appearing in print, so I'll have to thank them anonymously. The un-anonymous people whose names appear below (in no particular order) were extraordinarily helpful, and none of them are responsible for my mistakes. The anonymous people are responsible for those.

I'm grateful for the time and observations of Ned Johnson and Leah Adams at PrepMatters; Sam Schulman and Elizabeth Clark; Michele Rodriguez; Bruce Poch at Pomona College; Bill Tingley, Eric Newhall, and Marcia Homiak at Occidental College; Ed Fiske of the *Fiske Guide*, Lloyd Thacker of the Education Conservancy, and Robert Sternberg at Tufts University; Paul McHugh and Joseph Epstein; Bob Schaeffer, Bob Morse, Kat Cohen and the staff of IvyWise; and the fearless Rebecca Zwick of the University of California.

Speaking of fearless—I wouldn't want to be the person who has to start Richard Vedder's car every morning. He and Dan Bennett of the Center for College Affordability & Productivity raise questions and do research that few others in their field will raise or do. Ben Wildavsky read drafts of three chapters, and though I think he disagreed with nearly every word, he offered constructive criticism with his usual care and good humor. Ken Kleinfeld showed me the innards of a test-prep course and spent long hours teaching me how the business works, though my SAT score is my fault and not his. I'm grateful also to Scott Jaschik, coeditor of the splendid web site Inside Higher Ed; the sunniest thing I can say about higher education in the United States is that there's hope for any industry that has Scott policing it.

Kari Barbic and Emily Schultheis applied their invaluable corrective touch to the manuscript. Not one but two editors at Simon & Schuster provided indispensable guidance: Colin Fox nursed this book along the highway to publication and Priscilla Painton knocked it over the finish line, saving me from many awkward turns of phrase, bad jokes, and mixed metaphors. (I have to remember to have them read over these acknowledgments.) Glen Hartley and Lynn Chu, of Writers' Representatives, combine to create the ideal agent, with a one-two punch that strikes fear into the stony hearts of publishers and inspires gratitude in the trembling heart of a writer. John Podhoretz, Peter Berkowitz, Ed Whelan, Nick Gillespie, Patrick Cooke, Leon Kass, and my colleagues at the *Weekly Standard*—especially Claudia Anderson, Matt Labash, Bill Kristol, Terry Eastland, Vic Matus, and Jonathan Last—were quick with encouragement and good sense. And my thanks to Nick and Mary Eberstadt, Michael and Jenny Cromartie, Leslie French and Rame Hemstreet, Becky Blood and Giovanni Snidle, Richard and Liz Starr, Paul Lindblad and Jo Ann Innes, P. J. and Tina O'Rourke, Philip and Grace Terzian, Karen Kelser and Kahlid Hamami, David and Darcy Tell, and all their nearly flawless children, for their jokes, friendship, conversation, and, in the parents' case, liquor.

And finally to my family: my father, who may be surprised to see where all his tuition money went thirty years ago, my brothers Stan and Rick, and my wife Denise. Without her there would be no Gillum and Emily, to whom this book is dedicated, with love.